The Edge of Greatness

Joni Woelfel

Resurrection Press
An Imprint of
CATHOLIC BOOK PUBLISHING CO.
Totowa • New Jersey

First published in September, 2004 by

Catholic Book Publishing/Resurrection Press

77 West End Road

Totowa, NJ 07512

Copyright © 2004 by Joni Woelfel

ISBN 1-878718-93-2

Library of Congress Catalog Card Number: 2004106632

Cover art by Mary Southard, CSJ, © 1997 Sisters of St. Joseph of LaGrange

Design by Beth DeNapoli

Printed in the United States of America

1 2 3 4 5 6 7 8 9

Dedications

I dedicate this book to my friend,
and colleague, Adolfo Quezada.

—Joni Woelfel

We dedicate our commentaries to the
Radical Love of Father Greg Tolaas.

—Joseph and Sheila Biernat

Acknowledgments

I AM grateful to the editors of the following publications for permission to reprint chapters of this book which were originally published there.

ACTA Publications (www.actapublications.com)

"The Legacy of a Leopard Coat," which appeared as "Over the Fence," in *The Light Within: A Woman's Book of Solace*, 2001.

Catholic Women's Network

"Beyond the Silence"

"Long Live Annie Oakley"

"Lost Love Found"

"Reservoirs of Faith"

"Sacred Space on the Internet"

"The Shadow of Depression"

"What Happens When We Say Yes"

"What Our Hearts Become"

"The Ugly Duckling"

National Catholic Reporter (www.NCRonline.org)

"Blessed Be the Peacemakers," which appeared as "Cruelty and Comfort in Stray Cats' Lives," April 5, 2002.

"Fear, Faith and a Snake," which appeared as "Fears and Faith in the Weeds," September 6, 2002.

"The Violins of Autumn," which appeared as "Autumn's Golden, Poignant Days," October 4, 2002.

"Exodus to the Light," November 15, 2002.

"The Glory of Stillness," which appeared as "In the Shade at Grandma's," February 21, 2003.

Stauros Notebook

"The Final Lesson," Volume 21, Number 3, Autumn, 2002.

Contents

Preface: Mentors in Hope

FROM birth to death, we are on a spiraling journey to come into the fullness of our true selves. Our relationships and life experiences are our teachers as we evolve, transform, resurrect and integrate the precious facets that make us who we are.

We are not meant to come into this fullness alone. Coming into our true selves requires earnest willingness to process our challenges remembering that only what we bring to the light and acknowledge can be healed. As we embrace our hidden and disinherited voices, we own our shortcomings and life's hurts—and the power comes.

This abiding, magnificent, glorious power is the birthright of every human being. Individually and collectively, we stand on the edge of a new consciousness that is holy and authentic, ringing out with clarity in the hearts of all who walk the way of peace, compassion, inclusion and wisdom. What we learn and discover—and in turn give—becomes a sacred offering upon what is the altar of our lives. Through this intimate bond, we find ourselves commissioned as mentors in faith and empowerment.

In her ardent call to humanity Macrina Weiderkehr writes, "If you want to know if you are good for others, ask yourself how much hope you've given them. We need so desperately to learn how to hope more completely in all those little bits of life scattered through our days. We need to be so very careful lest we throw someone away because of our lack of hope in their potential, their possibility to be." As people living on the edge of this pivotal time in history, God is asking us: *How life-giving are you?* And within our desire to reach out to others that question also haunts us about ourselves. "Loving ourselves is the missing link in the divine plan," Adolfo Quezada writes in his groundbreaking book, *Loving Yourself for God's Sake*. With this thought in mind, we are ushered into a new freedom that elevates us to our highest good and highest potential.

This book represents a sacred offering from the altar of my own life and that of others—in the hopes that it will serve as a companion and guide to men and women from all walks of life who are deeply involved in the journey into fullness of being. Let us walk together in the brilliant light portrayed by the cover artist, echoing May Sarton's poetic words "Now I Become Myself":

> All fuses now, falls into place
> From wish to action, word to silence
> My work, my love, my time, my face
> Gathered into one intense
> Gesture of growing like a plant.

With great love and hope, I affirm your call to empowerment.

Joni Woelfel

Part One

Living as a Voice

A voice says, "Cry out!" And I said, "What should I cry?"
                                                    —Isaiah 40:6

When I dare to be powerful—to use my strength in the service of my vision—then it becomes less and less important that I am afraid.   —*Audre Lorde*

Do not be afraid of greatness; some are born great, some achieve greatness and others have greatness thrust upon them.
                                        —*William Shakespeare*

Each time anyone comes into contact with us, they must become different and better people because of having met us. We must radiate God's love. We must know we have been created for greater things.   —*Joseph Campbell*, Follow Your Bliss

~ 1 ~

—❦ What Happens When We Say Yes: ❦— Saying Yes

. . . every one of God's promises is a "Yes."

For this reason . . . we say the "Amen," to the glory of God.   —2 Corinthians 1:20

A NUMBER of years ago, I had an unexpected but valuable experience. It was a day like any other—until I opened the envelope with no return address and unfolded a neatly typed letter that came in that morning's mail. It began with my name misspelled and without a date. It was the first criticism of a column I'd been writing for over a decade.

My hand was shaking slightly by the time I'd read it. The letter writer vehemently disagreed with one of my heroines, who is one of the most respected feminine voices in the Catholic church and the world today, who stands up for spiritual equality for women. This heroine had written me a consoling letter, following the death of our son, and asked me to be a fellow Light Bearer. With tears streaming down my face and into my computer keyboard, I had written her back, "Yes, yes . . . yes."

Distressed, I wrote to a handful of mentors who are well-known writers. One responded, "It seems that when a person has found her heart and voice, it is inevitable that she will not be cheered by everyone. You are now that person! There are those whose "controlled world" will be threatened . . . and whose only way to respond is to judge and condemn. It is true for the person you wrote about and now it is true for you. If you have the courage to live from your heart here at the edge of a new consciousness where we live today, you will be a challenge to others. Welcome to this uncomfortable place." Another wrote, "Any letter that is anonymous goes into the trash. Anyone who won't sign a name is not worthy of your time in reading it." Still others humorously wrote, "Join the crowd; you must be doing something right. If you can't take the heat, don't publish." And lastly, the shining woman of courage who had been blasted in the letter wrote me, "Congratulations. If we are ever going to do anything of value at this step-over time in history, we are going to have to say first what is not permitted to be said at all . . . *it will be all right. Trust God.*"

What a rite of passage! I took the letter that blasted the heroine and made it into an artistic collage that I proudly display. On it are pasted the encouraging words of the mentors and leaders who advised me. The collage serves to remind me that being a voice and standing up for what we believe is a serious privilege. Knowing where we stand fills us with confidence when dissension comes. I also learned that leaders need affirmation and a sense of kinship when confronting issues.

Becoming a leader and living a life of service is a profound honor and responsibility which takes time and patience. It is amazing what happens to us when we say yes, but it's even more amazing when we, in turn, can support and invite others to be another voice of hope.

God Who Knows All the Answers, your guiding words for survival of the soul when we don't know where to turn

or what to do are: "Say Yes to the light. Carry the light.
Lead others where the light has led you. All will be well."

He Said

Serving as a member of the city council in a large metropolitan area, we often had to make incredibly critical votes. Our thirteen-member council was philosophically split, so 7-6 votes were common. Think about the importance of that seventh and deciding vote: it determined if a skyscraper got built, if thousands of municipal employees had their labor contract approved, if heavy industry expanded on the riverfront or if cleanup for housing and open space took place instead.

These 7-6 "cliffhanger" votes were tense because there was one member who rarely revealed his position until the time of the vote. Knowing it was 6-6 and that he was the deciding vote, he was lobbied ferociously. And just when we thought we were winning him to one side or the other, he would shut his office door and be unavailable the final hours before the meeting. Frustrated, one day I lashed out at his aide, inquiring as to why he was never available before meetings. "Oh," she said, "that's his time with God." That was when he reflected, prayed and listened to God. Stunned, I wondered how many of us fail to communicate with God before we make a big decision. How many of us give in to pressure or act impulsively, only to regret it later? By saying "yes" to God, we place the power we are given in its proper place. *—JPB*

She Said

In August 2001, while watching the six o'clock news, I froze at the words I heard, "due to budget cuts, the Minneapolis Public Schools will be closing six schools . . . Bottineau Early Education Center . . . as being proposed at the school board meeting this afternoon." Instinctively, I cried aloud, "NO!" They could not close my son's school—it was one of the best programs in the city! I felt betrayed, angry, helpless.

Shaking my head in disbelief, I caught my reflection in a hallway mirror and a voice from within demanded, "What are you made of? What are you going to do?" Bustling out of the house, I drove to the school board meeting just blocks away and earnestly requested to know the reason for Bottineau's closure. It turned out to be the $73,000 annual lease fee *with no consideration of the quality of this tenured program.* Prayerfully channeling my anger, I worked with parents, teachers, community folks and our local government for several months to save Bottineau. After many meetings, letters and even a demonstration march from the school, Bottineau was given space in a district-owned building. Throughout this fight, I realized that often we can and do make a difference. —*SGB*

Work Book Page

Discussion or Journal Questions

1. Talk about a time when you knew you were meant to speak up and didn't. How did this make you feel and what did you learn from the experience?

2. Share a memory of someone who spoke up in your defense when you needed support or a time when you needed a voice and received only silence. How could this motivate you in a positive way?

Goal

To be more confident in believing that what you have to communicate is important, needed and wanted by God and the world.

Task

There are multi-dimensional, unique ways for each of us to be a voice through our natural abilities, talents and gifts. Some of these avenues include art, writing, music, dance, photography and others. Consider a concern you have at this time. Express what is on your heart, asking God for guidance to make a difference in the matter. Imagine what God would suggest and be open to confirming coincidences that will come into your life.

Remember that we are always called to be a voice through the empowerment of prayer.

Prayer Image

A child with tape over his or her mouth.

Affirmation Statement

I am gloriously created to express myself and to make a difference in healing the world.

~ 2 ~

❖ The Ugly Duckling: ❖
Living Powerfully

. . . your body is a temple of the Holy Spirit . . .
—1 Corinthians 6:19

WHEN I think of the human body as sacred, what comes to mind is an image of my beloved Grandma. She was what one would call pleasingly plump, fleshy in the most huggable of ways, her face full of folds and wrinkles. She was soft, like well-worn flannel, but her legs were extremely bumpy from varicose veins. As a child, I'd felt embarrassed when a town boy with no manners had exclaimed, *"What's wrong with your Grandma's legs?!!"*

The memory of that impolite, long-ago remark comes back to me as I reflect upon my own "thing to be pointed at . . . " a face permanently paralyzed by a medical condition called Belle's Palsy following surgery for Meniere's disease in 1996. In researching this topic on the Internet, the first thing I read was, "Facial impairments or deformities are one of the most devastating things that can happen to a person, producing low self-esteem and deeply affecting the person's psyche." Indeed, I thought, says who? I was looking for sites that offered uplifting advice, but what I found was about three million sites for plastic surgery.

I did find solace in something Clarissa Pinkola Estes writes in *Women Who Run with the Wolves.* "When women are relegated to moods, mannerisms and contours that conform to a single ideal of

17

beauty and behavior, they are captured in both body and soul, and are no longer free. Women have good reason to refute psychological and physical standards that are injurious to spirit . . . It is clear that the instinctive nature of women values body and spirit far more for their ability *to be vital, responsive and enduring* than by any measure of appearance. This is not to dismiss who or what is considered beautiful . . . but to draw a larger circle that embraces all forms of beauty, form and function." This perspective is clearly as important for men as it is for women.

When I looked in the mirror for the first time following surgery for Meniere's disease and saw my melted-looking face, I was horrified. I saw the same shock reflected back to me in the eyes of family, doctors and friends who saw me for the first time. Eventually, though, as we all got used to it, I made peace with letting go of how I used to look and fear of judgment by others. While something I would never have chosen, it has brought many gifts. I realize how fleeting and transient our 'looks' are and how important nurturing the inner spirit is. Although some people would be surprised that a person could have self-confidence and good self - esteem with a facial condition like this (I never call it a flaw), my question is: *Why not?* There are so many things that bring satisfaction and zest to life: such as developing talents, helping others, loving friends and family and finding your passion. The more we can encourage and educate each other to embrace all forms of beauty, the more we'll understand the true scope of the body as sacred.

As a young girl, I loved *The Ugly Duckling* by Hans Christian Andersen. In this universal tale, a mother duck hatches a baby who does not look like the other ducklings. He is ungainly, distinctly different and considered ugly. Cast out and overcome by rejection, he runs away and through mishaps learns many things. The ugly duckling longs to be free and lovely like the graceful white birds overhead. In the end, he finds he is indeed, a swan. Commenting on the story, Pinkola writes, ". . . the ugly duckling of the story is symbolic of the wild nature, which, when pressed into circumstances of little nurture, instinctively strives to continue no matter what. When an individual's particular kind of soulfulness, which is both an instinctual and a spiritual identity, is surrounded by psychic acknowledgement and acceptance, that person feels life and power as never before."

Dazzling, Ancient God of the Universe, we spiritually come of age when we come home to the true character of beauty.

He Said

Helen is in her late sixties, living in the same house since 1972. It is an old duplex in a neighborhood full of tired housing and high crime. A large woman, Helen has scoliosis, making walking difficult and painful. Her small living room is filled with fifty-eight framed pictures of children, leading one to believe these were Helen's children or grandchildren. But *fifty-eight?* "These are my babies and I am so proud of all of them," Helen beams with a smile and twinkle in her eyes. I soon learn that the fifty-eight children are not Helen's biological children—but they all have this in common: they are her foster children, many with brain disorders; raised and loved by Helen over a thirty-year span.

Sad as it is, many ugly ducklings in our society would end up abandoned except for the Helens among us who like God judge our hearts, not our looks or abnormalities. To truly live powerfully, we must see all people, including ourselves, through the eyes of Christ. —*JPB*

She Said

In the late 1970s, our female foursome followed a band named "Chameleon." Now twenty-five years later, we were gathering at Jeanie's house, an hour out of the city. Although all three of us had remembered our cameras to capture this yearly jaunt, when the time came Jeanie screwed up her face and pleaded, "No, I'm fat . . . and feel ugly. I don't want any pictures." We did not say a word. Jeanie had put on a few extra pounds, and we could all relate to that "fat, ugly feeling."

As we conversed, Jeanie described her horrific year: she had lost her job when her place of employment folded, her mother had had a heart attack and her mother-in-law had Stage 3 cancer. Externally, Jeanie looked tired, worn-out and heavy with life. As I listened to her though, I realized that internally she had an incredible resilience. She had switched jobs and was proving herself; she continued to be the bread winner of her family of four and she was current on her house payments, a house she had purchased on her own four years earlier. Plus, she had the wherewithal to connect with friends and talk over the old and new times—something vital to our spiritual health. Her beauty lies in this resilience and desire to survive and give when she is able. Although I don't have a snapshot of the day—forever in my mind is the picture of a maturing woman who is coming into her own. —*SGB*

Work Book Page

Discussion or Journal Questions

1. The foundation of the famous Jesuit priest Anthony De Mello's lifelong work was waking people up to the reality of their greatness. Keeping this perspective in mind, talk about a time when you felt ashamed of how you looked or when you were in the presence of another who was shamed or ridiculed. Imagine you can go back in time. As a voice of wisdom, what words of enlightenment and compassion could you offer?

2. In *Care of the Soul* Thomas Moore writes, "As we become transparent, revealed for exactly who we are and not who we wish to be, then the mystery of human life as a whole glistens momentarily in a flash of incarnation." Who is someone you admire and know personally who portrays inner beauty and why? Offer some thoughts on what it means to be transparent.

Goal

To be more aware of shallow, narrow perceptions of beauty—and to not let it define worth in yourself or others.

Task

Make-overs are very popular these days. People enjoy reinventing themselves by changing their looks and their homes. Pretend that you are going to make-over your spiritual life. What are three new areas you would like to explore further (meditation, taking a study class) and what are three things that have always grounded your faith that you want to affirm and re-dedicate? List them on a piece of paper and put it in your Bible or a book that has special meaning.

Prayer Image

A naked, newborn baby who has just entered the world.

Affirmation Statement

I am born beautiful and I will live and die with a sacred preciousness that needs no enhancement to make me more special.

~ 3 ~

⟶✸ Long Live Annie Oakley: ✸⟵
Paying Attention

Those who are wise shall shine like the brightness of the sky, and those who lead many to righteousness, like the stars forever and ever. —Daniel 12:3

WHEN I was a child growing up in the 1950s, I truly wanted to be Annie Oakley when I grew up. I wanted to ride the range, live on horseback, watch blazing sunsets by a campfire and sleep in a tent with a hole in the roof so I could see the stars. I ran barefoot everywhere until the soles of my feet were like leather. Wild girls, like Annie Oakley, I reasoned, certainly didn't wear shoes—unless you were wearing cowgirl boots (in my case, a mended pair of hand-me-downs from my cool cousin, Butchie, that I thought were the living end, to wear with my pink and white cowgirl jacket).

All cowgirls must have a horse, so I went into Dad's old shed and dragged out a saw horse. Taking some beat-up lumber scraps, I nailed a neck and head on it. Then, I scrounged under the sink and cut up some old white rags for a mane and tail and pounded in two large, penny nails for ears. Even now, all these years later, I can remember the elation I felt when I was six. That horse seemed real in my imagination, and life was saturated with magic, dreams to come true and exciting horizons I couldn't even name yet. I was as fearless as Annie Oakley, spunky, resilient and a free spirit.

Later, as I reinvented my life through a framework of illness, grief and passing the half-century mark, I wondered how such a trusting child could grow up to have so many fears. I wondered how I could have forgotten all the truths that I instinctively knew as a child—and that were epitomized by my heroine, Annie Oakley. Annie was a legend, a beloved icon, an American original. She toured with Buffalo Bill's Wild West Show, performed on Broadway and was acclaimed throughout the world. As a fatherless, abused, poverty-stricken child, she grew up to become a strong advocate for women during World War I; and in an age when there were few options for women other than homemaker, she was a true trailblazer who opened doors and instigated a new image for American Women. She was well known as someone who stood up staunchly for her beliefs, but her reputation was also that of a respectful, thoughtful, wise and loving individual, reflecting her family's Quaker faith.

I think Annie's adventurous voice, wisdom and spirit live on in the hearts of all whom she inspired—men and women alike. Her legacy still exhorts us to remember what we always instinctively knew growing up—things like, you should view the moon and stars every night, and:

- When the wind rolls through the tall roadside grasses like an ocean wave, it is God passing through.

- When the summer snow from the cottonwood trees floats in the air, love is reminding us to be gentle with ourselves and others.

- When we hear a crow caw, it is God reminding us to pay attention to the world we live in and the voices that call us to our highest, most confident selves.

- When we marvel at the iridescent sheen on a dragon-fly wing, that beauty is there as a message to remind us how intricate, delicate and detailed life is, if we only take the time to notice synchronicities and balance in our lives.

- When we see a majestic, purple cloud bank burgeoning before a thunder storm, it is nature's voice reminding us to stay strong and to worship the God who made us and protects us.

There is no shame to be felt for the times we have forgotten these inherent truths that are there to sustain and comfort us, but rather, compassion for the reasons (too much stress, tragedy, illness, injustice and heartache) should fill our hearts as they do God's. Annie would have understood. Through the sunsets and wild things that can never be tamed, one can imagine her wisely saying, "Hold your head high, cherish your precious, sacred life . . . take risks, try new things, don't listen to voices that want you to live small, narrow or petty lives. Live a glorious life that blesses and gives your heart the wings it was meant to have." Wise Annie, we still hear you, we still love you . . . and we still follow your star.

God of the Morning and Evening Stars, you rise and set in our hearts each day, calling us to adventure and confidence through unfamiliar and challenging experiences as we widen, deepen and expand our horizons.

He Said

Sometimes we wonder "What if . . . " What if I would have traveled more, pursued more schooling, took the job I was offered?

Where would I be today? In his mid-twenties, my brother-in-law, Gary decided he would delay marriage and experience the world. That was three decades ago and the lanky man with movie-star looks is still single, but has a unique knowledge and appreciation for nature, the world's environment, different cultures and the wonders created by God. One needs to only ask once, and Gary will instantly set up a slide projector and share his pictures of Antarctica, Alaska, Belize, New Zealand and other far-off lands. And he has more pictures of sunsets and penguins than *National Geographic.*

"Never take nature for granted," is a strong warning from this man who helped clean the shorelines after the Valdez oil spill in Alaska; who worked with scientists in the South Pole, where the sun hides for six months a year, leaving total darkness and sub-zero temps. Gary's globetrotting has stopped for awhile as he earns his doctorate degree in physical therapy at the University of Montana in Missoula. But whether it be the mountains, the sun-set, the ocean or the human body—we are all surrounded by the wondrous works of our Creator. Acknowledging that is key to a full and rich life.   —*JPB*

She Said

Working as a paralegal in an insurance company law depart-ment, the best phrase that describes our common goal was "avoid risk." Perhaps that explained my side search for adventure. Luckily, I found it through the women's group at work. In the late 1980s many corporations encouraged women's groups to flourish, there-by proving their tolerance of diversity in their all-male hierarchy. As the Twin Cities "Women Who Dare" group, five corporate women's groups planned an event for a large audience of women.

But who would be our first speaker? And what would she talk about? Driving home one evening, I heard about Ann Bancroft and her North Pole trek as the sole woman with seven men. As a child, she had overcome dyslexia to be a teacher and now was doing what no woman had ever done. Perfect!

Although we didn't have much of a budget, we believed people would want to hear Ann, so we booked a room at the Minneapolis Convention Center and prayed that tickets would sell. And sell they did! Ann was an amazing speaker, telling us all we wanted to know and more—the challenges of the trip physically and mentally being the lone woman among seven men, dealing with 'female issues' of monthly cycles and hormones, the 120° below wind chill, etc. The only part we envied was her unlimited calorie intake, sticks of butter and all. The greatest thrill for me, however, came at the end of the evening when she turned to our group and acknowledged that daring takes all kinds of forms and that she admired the courage it had taken us to sponsor an event with an unknown outcome. Annie Oakley would have loved Ann Bancroft!   —*SGB*

Work Book Page

Discussion or Journal Questions

1. Recall one of your earliest childhood memories that remains a touchstone for you of well-being, adventure and the sacredness of life. If this memory had a message, what would it be?

2. If you were to spontaneously share an unresolved fear from the past that you have carried for a long time, what comes to mind?

Goal

To recognize, acknowledge, give voice to and bless wounds and fears from childhood and past experiences that hold you back.

Task

Deep within ourselves, there is a sacred, inner wildness that can't be tamed or fettered by burdens, injustice or life's demands. In this holy, authentic space, we respond to the call to be wild and free, trusting the spiritual language of our instincts. This does not mean that we set aside our responsibilities but rather empower them.

What ways and experiences best connect you with nature? Make plans to regularly deepen this bond by visiting a park, going for a walk, prayerfully observing the sky and noticing the sights, sounds, smells and weather of the outdoors.

Prayer Image

A lone wolf howling from a cliff to a full moon.

Affirmation Statement

In order to live gloriously, I must pay attention to the language of nature and the inner prompting within that wants all parts of me to be free and holy.

✤ Beyond the Silence: ✤
Being for Others

. . . whatever the Lord says to me, that I will speak.
—1Kings 22:14

IF someone asked you this very minute who your personal heroes and heroines are, who would you name? Joseph Campbell, mythologist and philosopher, once wrote, "Original experience has not been interpreted for you and so you've got to work out your life for yourself. The courage to face the trials and to bring a whole new body of possibilities into the field of interpreted experience for other people to experience—that is the hero's deed. Life is pain, but compassion is what gives it the possibility of continuing."

When I think of my own heroines who have resurrected and reinvented themselves following fragmentation and upheaval in their lives, among many, I think of Sr. Ave Clark. I've wanted to tell her story for sometime, this valiant woman who has inspired me to speak the deepest and truest truth. Her story is nothing short of remarkable—human and sacred—and it is an honor to tell it. When I feel intimidated or as if presenting the full truth of my experiences is too 'outside the box' of what is acceptable, I remember our friend, Sr. Ave Clark, O.P. from Bayside, New York, who has a retreat ministry called Heart to Heart. Author of the compelling book *Lights in the Darkness: For Survivors and Healers of Sexual Abuse,* Sr. Ave has two aspirations which are a driving force in her ministry: to extend comfort to others and to educate. She speaks out from the silence and this is her story.

Sr. Ave contacted me to say that her group was using my book *Meditations for Survivors of Suicide* in a retreat. I was touched by her reaching out to me—a complete stranger—and as time passed, we communicated more deeply. In her book, Sr. Ave writes in the dedication, "I am a survivor of abuse (incest, rape and sexual assaults). One cannot dare to say these brave, painful words alone. One needs courageous and faithful companions to be with you in the terrible darkness . . ." Sr. Ave's story reflects her finding the support she needed and out of this journey of woundedness, extending the power of consolation and the love of God to others through her many ministries (including those who suffer from Post Traumatic Stress Disorder, which she understands well). Her community of Amityville, NY Dominican sisters has been especially caring, Sr. Ave says. She lost several close friends on 9/11 and even though her heart—like so many others—was broken, she reached out and continues to reach out to the hurting people of New York. In her book, she says, "Solidarity is the reality of human existence and its first hope for survival." Out of wounds transformed, Sr. Ave encourages all human beings to "get in touch with that which holds us imprisoned and to be free."

Sr. Ave encourages those who have known tragedy to step forward and become "Pilgrims of Grace, immersing themselves in the journey of healing life's deepest wounds, discovering new paths, creating new friends and finding new ways to celebrate life." Through her gentle fidelity to offering the truth and being a light of comfort, I was inspired to follow her light as I developed my own ministry for survivors of suicide following the death of our son. Through Sr. Ave's example, I came to see where the strength lies to endure in this work that I love. She explains in her brochure, "Ministry is not done 'for people' as much as something done 'with people.' Go out into the darkness . . . and put your hand into the hand of God, trust greatly. It is more important to be compassionate than successful. The best ministry begins where faith and life meet."

As our troubled planet reels from ongoing tragedies and injustices of many kinds, more than ever, we need role models like Sr. Ave, who compassionately call us forth to do our work. "There is no painless way. But there is in this holy journey a sacred space that we will rediscover when we learn to trust again. The brightness of the light of love of others and of ourselves will invade the turmoil and enable us to hope and believe in the resurrection now. To seek resurrection actively is what the grieving process in recovery is all about. God offers us life." According to Sr. Ave some people come into our lives and leave footprints on our hearts called compassion and that, after encountering them, we are never, ever the same. Sr. Ave Clark's legacy of love work has indeed left footprints that invite us to immerse ourselves in the beauty, comfort and meaning that can only be found through faith. To know her is a privilege, to be a fellow voice *beyond the silence* with her a joy.

God Who Always Stands By Us, thank you for reminding us that as we stand by others, being a voice in ministry at its highest level is always paired with compassion and unconditional respect.

He Said

My friend Jeff is an inmate in federal prison. Not long ago, this 35-year-old was a successful business man. When he was first imprisoned, Jeff felt lonely, isolated, and unwelcome. The coldness and harshness he initially felt was something he wanted others to avoid. First, however, he had to examine his own path, "Why am I here? Do I have a good heart? Was I a decent human being? What went wrong?" His period of reflection convinced him that he needed to rid himself of greed and self-righteousness. Wholeheartedly, he accepted Jesus and realized his imprisonment was God's way of getting his attention . . . it worked!

Jeff began working with others to create a non-denominational ministry called "A Better Way to Live" (abetterwaytolive.org), which today reaches tens of thousands. Now, Jeff is the first one to greet new prisoners and offer them a warm smile and tutorial on their new surroundings, later following up to make sure they are adjusting to prison life. He also invites other inmates to this ministry. Truly, no matter where we are, each day God gives us opportunities to reach out and make a difference in someone's life, to help them survive. Funny how it works though: reaching out to help others survive is really God's way of helping us survive.

—JPB

She Said

Many years ago, active in a United Way fundraising drive, I looked high and low for a phrase to capture the essence of volunteerism. Frustrated by what I found, I created one: "It is when we help others that we learn of ourselves." Time and time again, while reaching out to others, I received gifts far greater than any given.

Although she won't make a "Who's Who in America," my dear friend Florence was a heroine. With the utmost grace, while the aging process slowly took her physical abilities away, her spirituality surged. She trusted that God would provide and He did. A true heroine's quality is that she can still creatively lead while sitting down, and do it unbeknownst to those she's leading. Florence had the extraordinary talent of recognizing others' gifts. She would encourage, thank and praise us no matter how little or big the task. She also matched us up with what we did best: friend Diana, dog lover, took Florence's dogs to the vet and groomer; friend Ron, mechanic, did her car maintenance and grass mowing; friend Jim, gardener, pruned her trees and planted hostas; and I, the office worker, organized her bills, mail and took her to doctor appointments. Remarkably, the whole neighborhood came together to help Florence stay in her home until the Lord called her at age 87. To this day, we neighbors converse and remember her fondly. Florence had not only created a bond with each of us but an everlasting bond among us. —*SGB*

Work Book Page

Discussion or Journal Questions

1. Ministry is love work. This is our calling, no matter who we are, what has happened to us or how old or sick we get. Describe some of the love work you have been the recipient of in your life, as a result of someone else reaching out to you.

2. It has often been said that wherever our passion lies, there also lies our greatest potential for ministry work. What are you most passionate about? How does this inspire creativity in you and how do you see this translating and flowing into love work that you can offer someone else, your community or the world?

Goal

To deepen and define what ministry is and to explore its call.

Task

There are many ways to reach out to others and many avenues. Ministry work is an intimate response to life and God, unique to each of our circumstances. Teachers, janitors, plumbers, stay-at-home moms, farmers, hairdressers—no matter what profession we work in, we can embrace an attitude of ministry, when it is defined as a life perspective in all we do.

Talk about ways in which you would like to change how you view the call of ministry in your own life, work, relationships and faith.

Prayer Image

Two uprooted trees that remain standing by leaning against one another.

Affirmation Statement

I am called to the ministry of love-work all my life through the flow of my own passion, creativity, wounds transformed and wisdom gained.

~ 5 ~

⟶⇤ Sacred Space on the Internet: ⇥⟵
Standing for Integrity

*If it is possible, so far as it depends on you, live peaceably
with all.* —Romans 12:18

CONSIDERING the dependence we have on the Internet,
users should be aware of and honor the concept of sacred
space. Through an unsettling experience I had on an illness support website, I saw how a very good and helpful thing can be
destroyed by insensitive and cruel behavior. Julia Cameron,
author of *The Artist's Way,* writes that "creativity flourishes in a
place of safety and acceptance, grows among friends and with-
ers among enemies." I quickly learned that acceptance of people
who did not remotely think like I did was a must. However, the
impulsive, harsh words of one individual on a regular basis began
to get to me. Finally, a horrendous crisis arose and a number of
people were badly hurt.

I cared about this site very much. I'd made wonderful friends
there, learned many things and was provided with an opportunity
to extend care and have that care reciprocated in powerful ways.
However, as the lack of safety of expression on the site was lost, a
dark resentment mushroomed in me towards the combative individual; I felt there was a tremendous betrayal of goodness, conti-
nuity and sacred space by this person.

I found some consolation by reading *This Blessed Mess* in which
Patricia Livingston writes, " Discontinuity is a characteristic of reality. We must lose our primitive, archaic, childlike trust that nothing

bad will ever happen to us. We remain unformed if we are never forced to enter the reality of imperfection, thrown back deep into ourselves on resources of which we are only dimly aware. Betrayal can, in the end, be a blessing. Chaos and then . . . creation." With sadness and hope, a friend from the site and I decided to form a new community. Within days, my friend, Gary Frye had created and designed a beautiful new support site that flourished for over a year, until we moved on to co-creating two other sites reflecting our Mission Statement that light and safety were our foundation stones and that people from all walks of life were welcome. Most importantly, we stated that any comment considered cruel, frightening or attacking another person would simply be erased, thereby preserving the intent and integrity of our site.

The story does not end so simply or neatly, however. I found that maintaining sacred space within myself is hard to do when you view someone as an enemy. Holding someone out of your heart is draining and while it was not what I wanted to do, I realized that only forgiveness was going to restore my inner peace. Wisely said by Christiane Northrup, MD in *Women's Bodies, Women's Wisdom*, " I learned that forgiveness is organic and that it is physical as well as spiritual and emotional. I subsequently learned that the only way to heal the situation was to withdraw my energy from it and to forgive my accuser. *I learned that forgiveness comes unbidden, by itself, when we are committed to healing.*" As I began to inch toward compassion, being committed to healing was the one thing I could genuinely count on in myself. That and the knowledge that I never contributed to the pain of the person I resented. Because I was secure in the sacred spaces I was creating, my perspective widened and I began to seek generosity of spirit. I was able to acknowledge the emotional wounds and attitude disorder in the other person, who desperately needed to feel important, superior and in control. Finally, within this shift towards tolerance and psychological insight came one of the greatest gifts that rise through the power of sacred space: *the desire to be a peacemaker.*

> *God of Great Holy Wars and Untold Battles, to make a stand for integrity and inclusion without backing down and to persevere as a peacemaker when the other party wants no part of peacemaking remains one of your greatest commissions in us.*

He Said

We all need our space; it is a fact of life. Finding that "space" might be as simple as having some personal items near your computer station at work, or a place to reflect at home, or perhaps a small homestead in the country with no neighbors for miles. Space is important. But there is a difference between getting away and running away. No one knew this better than my grandfather.

An immigrant from the "old school," Papa Pete was the owner of a small dairy store (now called convenience stores). His secret to living a long, healthy life was his integrity and his ability to give himself space. Whenever things got tough and business was slow, he would head up to his small fishing shack for a day or two. Upon his return, he would be in a good mood, ready to tackle the issues of the day. Papa Pete was not running away from his problems, but he believed by getting away and removing himself from them temporarily, that he'd gain a better perspective and be better able to deal with his customers and challenges.

If we remember to view the world from God's perspective rather than our own, He will give us wisdom, knowledge and understanding. We can then face our situation refreshed, with an open mind. After all, even Jesus had to get away from the crowds and his disciples to pray alone to his heavenly Father, to receive insight and understanding. —*JPB*

She Said

To be a peacemaker, we need to decide which road to take: "acceptance" or "rejection." If we want to be a peacemaker, "acceptance" is key. My friend Nancy tried for months to figure out how to make her curmudgeonly 85-year-old friend Evelyn happy. Then one day, Nancy realized all God wanted her to do was love Evelyn. This meant allowing Evelyn's anger to ebb and flow, and not take it personally. When Evelyn realized that Nancy loved her regardless of her behavior, her heart softened and a transformation began. Eventually, Evelyn felt secure enough to share her feelings with Nancy, as well as her strong love of God and many verses of beautiful poetry she had written. When we choose "acceptance," we must open our arms wide and love others fully, aware that we may never totally understand or agree with the reasons behind their "why."

Six days before Evelyn died, I visited her at her home. Although weak with congestive heart failure, her mind remained remarkably focused. Evelyn knew she was dying and at one point our talk turned serious and I asked, "Evelyn, are you ready to go to heaven?" Her reply surprised me when she said, "Honey, I never had it so good." Thanks to Nancy's unconditional, unrelenting love, Evelyn had opened up her wounded self and healed over the past nine years through the balm of friendship. —*SGB*

Work Book Page

Discussion or Journal Questions

1. Being a peacemaker is never without self-sacrifice, yet it is the only true avenue to inner peace and liberation. When you think of public figures, saints of the church and men and women of scripture who were peacemakers, who comes to mind and why?

2. When Pope John Paul II beatified Mother Teresa on World Mission Sunday 2003, publicists wrote that she was a contemporary icon of goodness; her biographers also wrote of her spiritual journey and dark nights of the soul. Her conscious commitment to God each day was a driving force that gave her the empowerment she needed to go forward in faith, despite anguish. Talk about a time when you experienced deep anguish in choosing the high road. How did this experience change you?

Goal

To live mindfully, aware of choices that inspire, create and sustain integrity.

Task

My friend, Ann Poplawski once wrote, "Love is truth, love is action to improve our wrongs, love is trust and trust yields love." Make a list of spiritual practices that help and affirm you the most in actively walking the way of peace and integrity. Share these thoughts with a friend with the intention of receiving new insights through the exchange.

Prayer Image

The yellow brick road from the Wizard of Oz.

Affirmation Statement

Each day, as I prayerfully make conscious choices to follow the road of integrity, I will experience the empowerment of faith.

~ 6 ~

⟶✳ Blessed Be the Peacemakers: ✳⟵ Small Acts of Kindness

Do not fear, greatly beloved, you are safe.
Be strong and courageous! —Daniel 10:19

SEVERAL years ago on a very cold, dark and rainy night I flipped the light switch to our garage from inside our house. From there, I could look through a window to check if our cat's food dish was empty. As I switched on the light, I caught sight of a stray, starving cat eating out of the dish. It stared at me with riveting eyes— paused for flight—but still eating hungrily. I knew that if I even moved an inch, it would be gone in a flash because it did not know I was safe yet. It did not know that I do not throw stones.

All that winter stray cats found their way to us—ill, bedraggled, thin and mistrusting. Some migrated down from the town dumpster, some got lost having traveled too far from surrounding farm homes, and others were just dumped off, discarded when no longer wanted. At one time, we had four stray cats—a pair of striking tortoise shells and two others who thought they lived here. (Which they did, though it was their idea, not ours.) Foxy came as a kitten, angora gray with a white ruff and as afraid and starving as a cat can get. Starvation will always overrule profound fear and eventually, because of this, Foxy was soon eating out of our cat dish. It takes about two months for a cat who has known terror and never been tame to trust. That is about how long it took Foxy, who spent his days gazing attentively into our house through the window, finding pleasure in our very presence.

Louis is a sleek, black tomcat with yellow eyes. Near death, starvation finally drove him to our porch. His leg was mangled and completely raw to the white bone. We set out food and when we were not around, he would drag himself to it and eat. Eventually he grew fat, sleek and very entertaining. Because of his gentlemanly ways and because he is an old cat, we began letting him into the house for visits. I then discovered that he was de-clawed. We'll never know his story, but finding this out explained his many and terrible injuries. He cannot climb trees to protect himself from dogs and he cannot hunt for food. In a short time, I observed something disheartening about our friendly pair of Siamese house cats. When Louis comes in the house, they chase him. They don't get violent but they are bullies. I have to separate them because Louis can't defend himself, and I think they sense this and take advantage of it. However, with persistence on my part, they are learning to get along better and at least tolerate each other.

I often see the psychology of human nature played out in the stories of our stray cats. I see the need for a place to belong, the need for safety. . . and the terror experienced at not having it. I see what starvation (whether physical or of the soul) will do as a driving force and the boldness that can result from it along with the desperation of doing things that are otherwise not natural to do. When I think of the wars in the world and what they do to people, I don't have to look farther than our "cat dish for starving cats" to understand the basic principles of those who have and those who don't, of those who must fight to survive and most sadly, the bullies who have no concept of the plights or rights of others.

From my own small village in my own safe corner of the world, I hold these things to my heart. The cruelty in the world pains me. It makes me want to seek shelter because I fear it, both for myself and for others. But then I remember the joy of Foxy, sunning himself on top of an old soda pop carton, washing himself contentedly. We took good care of him for several years until he died from pneumonia. Because of our efforts, Foxy knew he was safe and didn't have to worry about the future.

> *Mentor God Who is Master of Compassion, may all human beings come to an understanding of how much difference small acts of kindness can make in the world—that we should not throw stones at each other and that being a peacemaker and protector on all levels is the highest calling and privilege there is.*

He Said

When it comes to disputes in the workplace, among friends, church, or family, do you ever feel like you should be wearing black pants and a black and white striped shirt with a whistle around your neck? I have never been comfortable being a referee although, ironically, I found myself in an awkward spot in my prayer group recently. Our prayer leader liked to pray for a variety of concerns, but another member continually asked us to pray for his Aunt Greta. One night the leader asked with exasperation, "Must we again pray for Greta? We've already prayed for her." His comment deeply upset this man and their dispute carried into the next day, with the dejected man relaying his anger to others from the group. When he spoke to me, I listened to him, nodded my head, but offered no position. In contrast, another member urged the two gentlemen to come together amicably, saying it was hypocritical to be praying with each other one day and arguing the next. His firm position promoted peace. The two members finally met and resolved their issue.

How many of us provoke hostility by agreeing with one or both sides? Rather than fanning the flames or being neutral, being a peacemaker takes courage and honesty. Do you picture Christ in a referee's uniform blowing a whistle or do you picture him wearing a robe of peace, hands stretched out to embrace us? Part of spiritual maturity means loving our neighbors and acting as Christ would. As the song says, "Let there be peace on earth and let it begin with me."

—JPB

She Said

Denise, a single Mom, once on welfare, gratefully remembers the assistance she received to go to secondary school and now gainfully employed gives back to her community ten-fold.

Last week, Denise called, angry and upset: "Someone broke into my garage and spray painted my new vehicle with graffiti!" This was just the latest of many acts of vandalism she had experienced during the past five years; now she was vowing to move. However, that evening she prayed and asked God what she should do. His answer led her to the house of one of the young graffiti "artists" the very next morning. As Denise approached the boy's mother, she noticed the woman's back stiffen when Denise mentioned that they needed to talk. Relief flooded over the woman's face as Denise inquired about having her son help Denise scrape her garage. The mother proudly called her son and they both became excited about the opportunity for him to earn some money. God showed Denise the path of the peacemaker.

—SGB

Work Book Page

Discussion or Journal Questions

1. We have all known bullies and we all have the potential to be a bully. However, bullies have the chance to become great humanitarians by learning from their mistakes—or remaining lifelong masters of cruelty.

   Talk about a time you witnessed cruel treatment of another. How did it make you feel? Did you confront the bully? Did you offer support to the one being hurt?

2. Talk about small acts of kindness you have experienced that gave you hope when you needed it the most. How does the memory of it continue to inspire you? Also, discuss a time when someone hurt you through ignorance (not knowing the truth or real facts) and a time when you said or did something that hurt someone else through ignorance.

Goal

To explore ways to make a difference in the world.

Task

Kent Nerburn writes in *Small Graces: The Quiet Gifts of Everyday Life,* "It is not our task to judge the worthiness of our path, it is our task to walk our path with worthiness." As you read this, who or what came to mind? This is a light shining on someone or something you need to be more attentive to. Talk about it, give it voice and make plans to remedy the situation in some way.

Prayer Image

A single spotlight on a dark stage.

Affirmation Statement

I will never underestimate the sacred power that performing small acts of kindness presents to affecting change and offering comfort to myself, others and the world.

War Through the Eyes of a Child: Inviting Peace In

I am for peace; —Psalm 120:7a

WHAT does war look like through the eyes of a child? If adults can't wrap their minds around the complexities of it, how can a child possibly make sense of it? In tackling this question, Adolfo Quezada asks, "How does the teaching of Jesus affect us as we respond to those who would be our enemies? Are we to demonize them and turn our people against them? Or, do we see our enemies as children of God on whom the sun also rises and the rain falls? Surely 'turning the other cheek' does not mean that we do not defend ourselves against aggression, but it does mean that we are to pursue peaceful means to the resolution of possible conflict as much as possible. Peace is more than the absence of war."

Many years ago, I wrote a children's fantasy story for our young sons as we all struggled to understand the frightening concept of war. The setting took place on a giant planet called Gumball, where the whole land was inhabited by jelly bean people made of every color you could ever imagine. Jelly beans were grouped according to color and jelly bean leaders—some dictators and some elected—were in charge of each group. Then, to take it all a step further, high, pillared chocolate walls were erected, to separate the colors. My sons drew pictures of all the jelly beans and colored them with crayons, as the story took root in their hearts. They could understand that the chocolate walls meant *"Keep out!"* as they grasped what the word *exclusion* meant.

As the story continued, jelly bean children curiously peered through holes in the wall at other jelly bean children, who were a different color than they were. It made my sons sad as wary voices would say, "No, no! They are not the same as us, they might lead you away from our truth; you mustn't wonder about other colors, ours is best!" This taught my sons what the word *segregation* meant. As the story unfolded, I wanted to bring hope as quickly as I could. "Many of the jelly beans and their leaders believed in the same Chief Candy Maker. They all tried very hard to live good lives out of devotion to the Candy Maker, who was creator of all jelly beans. These groups even sent ambassadors of good will to unhappy jelly beans behind chocolate walls across the ocean in the hopes that their warring planet could at last experience peace."

In the story, time passed and jelly beans came and went . . . and the chocolate walls never came down. In some places, the walls were piled even higher and guarded by militia. Immersed in the drama, my sons drew pictures of jelly beans in camouflage with guns and swords. One day, the Chief Candy Maker—filled with heartache by all the strife and division of the jelly beans— decided to design a very special jelly bean, to walk among all the jelly beans. He created this jelly bean in stripes, containing every color that every jelly bean had ever been made with. When he designed his heart, he took every flavor he had ever thought up and placed it at the center of this jelly bean. Then, he called this jelly bean his son. Many grew to love the striped jelly bean and multitudes began to follow him. It got to be too much for some jealous leaders and they had the striped jelly bean killed. My sons' drew endearing pictures of the striped jelly bean being put to death, as a word I wished they never had to understand became real to them: *crucifixion*.

However, the love spirit of the striped jelly bean was so strong, that he was more alive than he'd ever been and I wrote, "History was shaped by his coming and passing and his Love Spirit that couldn't die. But there were still black-hearted jelly beans who twisted the love messages and because they wanted power, built the chocolate walls even higher, trapping friendly jelly beans who wanted peace. The black-hearted jelly beans said their way was the only way and a terrible, devastating war broke out. My son's drawings depicted the battle with tanks, bombs and jelly beans waving white flags that pleaded, *"Please don't shoot."*

In the story, the Chief Candy Maker and the Striped Jelly Bean decided it was time to release mighty winds of change. They knew the Love Spirit, who lived in the hearts of all the jelly beans was the answer. And so they said, "Blow, Wind, blow across the whole land." And she did! What she caused was fire that did not harm. It began to burn in the hearts of jelly beans everywhere. It was a Fire of Tolerance, Inclusion and Compassion, and it began to melt the chocolate walls. Raspberry, lemon yellow, bubble gum pink and blueberry jelly beans began crossing over the walls that separated them and my sons colorful drawings portrayed their full understanding of the joyous event.

On every jelly bean they drew an insignia that said, *"Peace on Earth."* Far and wide, all across planet Gumball the word was out about the new insignia. It was received in many languages and proclaimed on striped banners of every color. The story ends, "Trust began to flourish on Planet Gumball, and there was so much mingling between the colors, that one day, there was a giant party to commemorate the raising of freedom flags all over planet Gumball . . . and they all lived happily ever after." If there is anything my sons understood, it was what it means to have a giant party and I still have their exuberant drawings all these years later to remind me. On the final page of my story, I wrote, "On Planet Gumball and in the hearts of all children who believe, the flags still wave to this very day, where they will stand forever to replace the chocolate walls." Through the eyes of children, beyond a doubt, this is how war would end. May their prayers and ours be heard.

> *God Who Dreams Peace Into Our Hearts, as adults, may we always remember that you call us to mature, childlike faith, never childish ways.*

He Said

On a sweltering August evening, the community hall was full with 50-60 area residents, angry and frustrated. At the front of the room stood the police precinct commander, trying to calm the upset crowd as he was bombarded with questions about the dramatic increase in drug and gang activity. "Make no mistake about it," he said, "we're living in a war zone right now." A little boy sitting next to his mother in the front row asked, "What's a war zone, Mommy?" Many parents at this meeting, holding their young and restless children weren't surprised with the label "war zone." They'd been enduring the apprehension, pain and suffering of an unsafe neighborhood, not so unlike the uncertainty that Afghan or Iraqi parents struggle with for their own children. They wonder, When will the fighting end? When will calm prevail?

A single mother, Rowina, tells the crowd of her summer respite, a one-night sleepover at a friend's home in a safe and a quiet suburban community on the 4th of July. She watched with pleasure as her two children played in the spacious backyard with her friend's children. All was well until a neighbor set off a series of firecrackers. As the firecrackers crackled and popped, Rowina looked in the backyard to see only her friend's children standing; her children had "hit the dirt" out of habit, believing that someone was shooting at them. War is so hard for children to comprehend; they innately desire peace. Let there be peace on earth and let it begin in our neighborhoods for the sake of our children.   —*JPB*

She Said

I listened with horror as my friend Saybah from Liberia recalled her life: at age 4 she was circumcised because her father's mother insisted on following tribal tradition. And at age 9, she witnessed the torture and murder of her father by rebel forces. These men were certain that her father knew where the government's money was, but he poignantly told them if he had known, he would have left long ago. He begged his persecutors to release his family, but they demanded that Saybah, her mother, her two brothers and sister huddle in a circle and watch as they repeatedly stabbed him.

She cannot get the picture out of her mind of her father clawing the ground like a chicken, desperate to hold onto his life, and calling out for Jesus (something she had never heard him do before).

After being rescued by a faction of soldiers, Saybah became a refugee and moved to four different countries before she came to the United States in 2002. She knows only a family divided: she has not seen or heard from her two brothers since leaving Liberia, and her mother and sister live in different states. She tells our bible study group that she has forgiven the men who killed her father, but she is not able to forget. She asks us to pray for peace for her country and for inner peace for herself. So much life and suffering for a mere child of 17. May God's grace sustain and uplift her!

—*SGB*

Work Book Page

1. Talk about someone who has betrayed you or someone close to you. How are you finding resolution and the grace to move forward?

2. Being able to dialogue about unpopular or opposing views requires maturity, reasoning, respectful listening and being able to agree to disagree. Talk about issues, topics and people with whom you have agreed to disagree. Have you ever felt hand-cuffed or obligated to someone you detested? What was the first small step that helped you detach?

Goal

To envision, believe in and work for peace, justice, tolerance and inclusion.

Task

Author and journalist Antoinette Bosco who lost her beautiful son and daughter-in-law to violent murder, writes in *Choosing Mercy: A Mother of Murder Victims Pleads to End the Death Penalty,* "I was honoring my murdered children by raising my voice against killing, all killing." While there are many who protest her views, Antoinette remains strong in her faith and convictions, inspiring all of us to seek peace and justice whenever possible.

Talk about a person you admire who inspires you to make a stand for the things you believe in. How does this person conduct him or her self?

Prayer Image

Christ crucified.

Affirmation Statement

I will look to Christ's life, death and resurrection when I am faltering and have lost my vision for empowered living and faith.

The Legacy of a Leopard Coat: Merging into Wholeness

I pray that you may have the power to comprehend,
with all the saints
What is the breadth and length and height and depth
And to know the love of Christ that surpasses knowledge,
So that you may be filled with all the fullness of God.
—Ephesians 3:18

ON my dresser, I have a photo of me taken in 1970 that I cherish. I am standing outside by our family car following a snowstorm, wearing my magnificent, mini-length faux (fake) leopard coat, high-heeled boots and holding my faux leather, dark brown vinyl purse with large gold zippers and a clanky chain handle that I thought was about as 'groovy' as you could get. My hair is long, blonde, straight and parted in the middle, in keeping with the fashion of the time. I look at the faded picture with the curled edges taken thirty-three years ago and I am amazed that I feel as young inside now as I did then. I still adore leopard print and *how I remember that coat!* Wearing it with its silky lining and turning the collar up made me feel energized, alive, gorgeous and empowered. It was like slipping on a persona that was the true me, in the fullest sense.

Now all these years later, I see a parallel between that glorious coat and the joy I have found in coming into the fullness of faith. I wouldn't trade it for anything, but it was a long, challenging journey—that I often refer to as crossing a fence. Years ago, during my early awakening days I wrote in *The Light Within*, " I sent a friend a card showing two children jumping over a fence, with a sign on it reading *no trespassing*. In the photo, the children are leaping over the fence as if it is the most natural thing in the world. I get a sense of great adventure beyond that fence—and the sense of an invitation to unexplored places in the image that has been off limits before. It makes me feel as if I really want to go there and wild horses could not keep me out or away!" This was written as I recovered from a bad experience in my life. As I healed, I indeed felt as if I'd crossed a fence because I saw life so differently. I was no longer intimidated by what I perceived as cultural or faith boundaries that shouldn't be crossed. I wanted to draw my own conclusions rather than question what I was taught or not taught by my traditional upbringing.

Because I didn't know where to turn, I traveled alone with no one to guide me at first, feeling my way in the dark, trusting and knowing I was changing. There was no stopping it. The only thing I didn't have was the validation and language for what was happening. I kept writing about being on the fringes, out there in no man's land, going wild and feeling drawn to feathers, rocks, rivers, trees, earthy colors, bawdy music like Ethel Merman belting out "Everything's Coming up Roses," exotic fabrics, spices and mystical books. I felt like I was unraveling and examining the belief strands that made up my life in its entirety for the first time. It was great.

There was also frustration, feeling that a major piece was missing that I didn't have a name for. I actually felt a bit rebellious, knowing that my search was drawing me to the study of a theology that would meet disapproval from certain people whose opinion mattered to me. Despite that, I began studying the feminine nature of God as well as the masculine. It was like coming home to myself, an "aha" moment that honored and blended beautifully with my love of God, as Father. Following this awakening in my life, I began to find a language that was my language. I began listening to my body, my feminine cycles, my intuition and trusting in the synchronicity of events and experiences—as the framework of my whole life began making sense.

I was like a child who had trespassed over a fence into a homeland that was mine to begin with. I had a whole new world to explore. Rather than detracting from my previous beliefs, it was as if they were uplifted, renewed, enfolded and energized. When I think of how coming into the fullness of integrated faith felt—I can describe it perfectly. *It was like slipping into my beloved, magnificent leopard coat . . . and the feeling has never left.*

> *God of Amazing, Techni-colored Dream Coats, the whole world, our precious spirituality—the very essence of who we are—comes alive with exuberance when we come into the fullness of gender-inclusive faith as men and women.*

He Said

I grew up during a time when two of the most popular television shows were "Father Knows Best" and "Leave It to Beaver." You know, shows where the mother vacuumed the living room floor in a pleated dress, pearls, and high heels; cheerfully greeted her husband hours later in another lovely outfit when he came home for dinner; and left all the disciplining for father. Thankfully, the home I grew up in was remarkably different. My mother raised six children while running her own grocery store. Dad had his own small business with no employees, making him a slave to his own joy. No doubt about it, in contrast to the popular television shows I was watching, Mom was the disciplinarian and head of the household. Her word was final and we all knew it. My close friends, as well as their mothers, were puzzled by our matriarchal household—it wasn't supposed to be that way.

I am so thankful for a strong, ambitious mother. It was a blessing to shut off television and know that the real world was different. I developed new and real impressions of women that were the antithesis of the subordinate stereotypes prevalent during this era. And today, I see an interesting contrast among me and my childhood friends who grew up in a "Father Knows Best" home. Many of these friends found mates coming from the same background and their households today mirror these TV shows of the past. I think about this often, usually while I'm vacuuming the living room, doing the laundry or loading the dishwasher.　　—*JPB*

She Said

As a young girl growing up Catholic, I loved the idea of having Mary, Jesus' mother, as someone whom I could turn to, pray to, and tell my innermost secrets to. It seemed perfectly natural for me to talk to her since my most comfortable bond was with my mother, not my father. My favorite place to pray to her was out in my Mom's garden, near the flowers (and we didn't even have the half-bathtub shrine to her). I also loved listening to the stories of Mary appearing to the poor children at Medjugorge, imparting to them important messages to deliver to the rest of the world, and the vision of her stepping on the snake as stars circled around her as she wailed aloud about to give birth to our Saviour.

I have been told by some Christians that it is idolatry to pray to Mary, so pondering this, I have come upon an idea that grants me great peace. I think of the three persons in God, the Trinity, as a family: God the Father; God the Son and God the Holy Spirit (Mother). The threesome makes up the divine family and gives homage to the male, female and child aspects of God, which he also manifested in all of us. To me, the Holy Spirit is the doer, the one that gets things done, the divine giver of gifts, and the one that helps us have a close relationship with God. It makes sense to me that the Holy Spirit is the feminine side of God, and that our loving God has provision for women in His kingdom and heart.

—*SGB*

Work Book Page

Discussion and Journal Questions

1. "The Rosary," Christin Lore Weber writes in *Circle of Mysteries: The Women's Rosary Book*, "is a mother prayer, and we are a world in need of a mother. We live so much in our heads. We feel beset with problems too big to solve. We need to find the mother within us, a living, acting compassion for all that exists. Mary is one mirror of that mother. The Rosary is her prayer; the Rosary practice makes us aware of her voice in our hearts."

   Talk about your memories of saying the Rosary or what you have observed from others close to you.

2. Recall a memory when your faith felt vibrant, alive and passionate. Describe how the fullness of faith feels to you.

Goal

To explore integrated, gender-inclusive faith.

Task

Christin Weber writes, "Some of my daughters say the world of men is cursed. They say it is time to return to the mother only; abandon Yahweh and return. I say no! This is not the time for further severing. This is the time to join. Our God is one. Mother-Father God is one. We divide ourselves. Now is the time for gathering."

Those of traditional faith and those of more progressive faith often find themselves at odds. This leads to needless dissension and anguish. Talk about what diversity, unconditional love and inclusion of faith means to you.

Prayer Image

The Holy Family.

Affirmation Statement

In the name of the Father, and of the Son and of the Holy Spirit, I honor the mothering nature of God with all my heart.

~ 9 ~

⟶⟩⟩ Walking in Fog: ⟨⟨⟵
Faith that Guides

For your steadfast love is before my eyes,
and I walk in faithfulness to you.   —Psalm 26:3

I'D forgotten what a presence fog has, until I went for a walk one Spring night. The fog had crept up silently, and when I stepped out into it unaware, I immediately felt a sense of heaviness, as if it were pressing upon me. I could barely see the street lights as I walked along the saturated gravel roads, skirting places where water pooled from the thawing of the frozen winter ground. Cold mud oozed up the sides of my sandals as with each step, my foot sunk in an inch or two. Just barely, I could make out the black silhouettes of the still budless branches of the trees, and as I tried to peer beyond the fog, I felt disoriented.

The fog seemed to shift in a barely discernible way, as if it were falling in upon itself in waves or drifts in the stillness. Our neighbor's dog, Sparky, started barking and the sound seemed louder and closer than usual, unable to echo across town because of the fog's containment. Pausing, I glanced up at the night sky, surprised to see that above the fog, I could see the clear, white moon perfectly, a steadfast presence of clarity that I did not expect to find.

I began to think of the fog that sometimes enshrouds and disorients the human heart. I thought of the elements in my own life that I do not envision the full scope and implications of—places where my memory is hazy. I remember a painful experience with such detail—even though that same experience is infused with shining things like the courage I have shown, or the glint of care in a glance from a loved one. Inaccurate, selective memory sometimes causes these beautiful things to elude me and as I walked, I resolved to be more aware of the non-life-giving reflections, that like the fog I was walking in, press upon me with a weight which I was never meant to carry.

In the spiritual realm, we sometimes can get lost in the fog, individually and collectively. Truths of the heart are present and always available, but only through faith can we draw upon their clarity. Long ago, one of my sons and I were driving home through fog so thick you could barely see the road. Our vehicle's headlights seemed to be absorbed into the tarred blacktop and three things stood out that I never would have noticed without the fog: the profile of my son's face beside me in the car, the sharp glow of the green dashboard lights and the white strips newly painted on the highway that guided our way. My awareness of "things close" was heightened in the fog as my grown son and I discussed what the experience felt like to us. He described it as a tangible, palpable embodiment of spirit that left him feeling uncertain and peaceful at the same time.

"What does that mean?" I asked.

Drawing a parallel between traveling in fog and traveling through life, he explained, "Both present but a hazy, nebulous glimpse of what lies ahead. Both can shroud danger and beauty and then lift at intervals to reveal reality." Fog to my son was a mystical experience that drew him to contemplation and a sense of secret adventure with hidden truths waiting to reveal themselves.

When all seems lost and unfamiliar, and indeed, the very planet seems to have lost its equilibrium, the whole world can seem disoriented. It is as if a fog has descended, shrouding justice, inclusion, mercy and goodness. Yet, during times of suffering, grief or trial—when we feel as if we are moving through fog unable to see what lies ahead—we have an opportunity to exercise heightened faith, solidarity, trust and authentic prayer unlike any other time. Like the moon shining above the fog, or the guiding white strips on the highway, *we understand more clearly than ever before that what lies closest to our hearts will be what guides us:*

> May vision of the highest order enlighten us,
> May compassion inspire us,
> May conviction uphold us,
> May reverence instruct us,
> May truth propel us,
> May empowerment bless us.

> *God of Steadfast Love and Devotion, may divinely-instilled clarity guide our decisions and paths through whatever we face, wherever we go, all the days of our lives.*

He Said

For a year, we had read about its enormity, studied its history, pictured it in our minds, and now it sat before us like a skyscraper casting a late afternoon shadow over a city. We had arrived! "Yes," we thought, "this was it, 'the great one,' the mountain they called 'Denali'." We had come upon a tourist lookout point and we could not move, we were totally enraptured by the grandeur of Mt.

McKinley, the highest mountain in North America—20, 320 feet! "Please take our picture!" we begged a passing hiker. It was a Kodak moment and we envisioned our next Christmas card with a backdrop of Mt. McKinley. He obliged and then suggested we come back when the full mountain was visible, that we were merely seeing the base of it, that fog was actually covering two-thirds of it. He explained that because of its massive size, the mountain creates its own weather and it is only visible about 20 percent of the time.

Fog, in non-weather terms, can be defined as something that prevents us from seeing clearly, or seeing the whole picture. The more we search, the more the fog is lifted revealing the unbelievable works of the Great I Am. Later in our trip, we were blessed with a rare day and we were able to see the mountain in full view. Although it is difficult to wait, we must remember it is God's timing that determines when the fog will be lifted and when his masterpiece will be shown. Wait upon the Lord and his mysteries will be revealed to you.   —*JPB*

She Said

"But I can't see!" I whined plaintively to my husband as we inched the old, worn Ford truck in the fog. The fog was opaque, as if someone had draped a gray flannel sheet over the entire vehicle. This was our first trip to Alaska and we were traveling from Glenallen to Valdez. Straining my eyes ahead, I insisted on pushing my hair away from my eyes, hoping that I could see more. "Keep praying and keep looking up!" my husband said tersely, his voice nervous as he navigated our way on a highway we'd never traveled. Praying was instinctive to me; I always prayed when I was really scared, but the "looking up" was foreign. Raised in the

Midwest, we looked to white lines on the side of the road as our guide in fog, snowstorms and rainstorms. Here, there were no white sidelines, no red-eyed tail lights in front, no bulging halogens behind (perhaps the natives knew better than to be out in this fog). The only guides were elbowed steel bars with white reflective tape spaced evenly *above* us. Hours later, we arrived exhausted and relieved. We started breathing again.

When we left Valdez a few days later, we humbly viewed what we had missed on the way down: cascading waterfalls such as Horsetail Falls, Bridgegroom Falls towering above us along one side of the road . . . and plunging canyons careening off the other side of the road. Perhaps most importantly we internalized a great lesson that day: no matter how much fog you find yourself in, "Keep Praying and Keep Looking Up!"   —*SGB*

Work Book Page

1. When people face the unknown through unexpected events, losses and changes in their lives, it is common to wish, "If only God would write me a letter that would guide me through this." We say, I can make it through just about anything, if I have the vision and support that I need. One of the greatest fears human beings have is fear of abandonment. Talk about a time when you had to venture forth into the unknown, not knowing how your life would end up. How did this change you?

2. Barbara Kingsolver wrote in her astonishing book *Small Wonder*, "God is in the details, the completely unnecessary miracles sometimes tossed up as stars to guide us. They are the promise of good fortune in a cloudless day, and the animals in the clouds; look hard enough, and you'll see them. Don't ask if they're real."

   Talk about small miracles you have experienced in your life that you carry close to your heart. These can include anything from seeing a butterfly when you felt shackled, greeting cards, dreams you have had, a song you heard on the radio. Talk about your thoughts regarding divine coincidence.

Goal

To trust faith as our guide when the future is unknown.

Task

When we must enter the unknown of our lives, it is prudent to not only rely on faith but to seek guidance through the counsel, inspiration and examples of teachers and mentors. When they offer their lives as a sacrifice poured out for the love of others, holding nothing back in their struggles and victories, we feel that when it is our turn to face the unknown, these persons are holding out their hands to us. Fr. Greg Tolaas was such a person. A beloved priest for the Church of St. Philip, Minneapolis, he was known for his persistent call to service, courage and inclusion. He lived with Cystic Fibrosis all his life and after a long and unrelenting, arduous battle, died September 7, 2003 from complications following a double lung and kidney transplant at the age of forty-seven. His parishioners, friends and family were devastated. Yet, even in their grief, they celebrated his legacy of faith, which sustained him through the unknown hope of the transplants to the hope of heaven. His unique life was a gutsy example of facing the unknown everyday of his life with faith, love, tears, a dogged honesty and passionate devotion to the Gospel. He could be irreverent, witty and reverent all at the same time, endearing him to all who knew him and called him friend. From the pulpit, he was described as articulate, brilliant and in touch with the times and people he served, his messages seemingly "custom built" for each person.

Talk about people you have known or admired who have served as guiding beacons of faith to you. As you face the unknown, whom do you consider counselors? If you do not have any, discuss someone you could ask, whether it be a priest, nun, professional therapist, parish leader, family member or friend.

Prayer Image

The Star of Bethlehem.

Affirmation Statement

When I must face the unknown, I see with new eyes as I learn to trust that I never walk alone. I am supported and aided by a heavenly host of spiritual voices and helpers.

~ 10 ~

A Chicken Names Elvis: Opening to Laughter

Now Sarah said, "God has brought laughter for me; Everyone who hears will laugh with me." —Genesis 21:6

"HEALING laughter," Jean Shinoda Bolen, M.D, writes, "is a relief from tension and an expression of joy and hilarity. At its most nurturing—which humor can be—there is an afterglow of good feeling. In the shared laughter, there is a sense of commonality about vulnerabilities and strengths."

I was born serious. Of the hundreds of articles I've written, I can count on one hand the number that are funny. Because of this, my humorous stories are important to me; I like to reread them from time to time, because I enjoy the silly grin I get on my face as I remember anecdotes like the following, written when our sons were young:

One day a hen at a local farmer's hen house decided to lay a nice, big egg. That egg, along with five others ended up on my kitchen table in an egg carton. The next morning, our son Dana brought the eggs to school where they were put in an incubator for a biology project. Every day, the eggs were misted, turned and carefully tended. Over a weekend, the magic thing occurred with no one to watch—no one to herald the hatching of one lone chick—and no mother hen to cluck in maternal tones, fluffing her feathers and warming the baby under her breast. Rather, there was the warmth of an electric light bulb.

The chick was named Elvis by our son and he quickly became a classroom celebrity. Fluffy yellow, constantly peeping, he was outgoing and tame from the moment he hatched. He would follow students around like a puppy, trotting along on his humongous feet. That chicken lacked for nothing. Curiosity got the best of me. I had to meet this Elvis. Dana brought him home for the weekend in a hamster cage. Peeping his head off, Elvis immediately gave the impression that he was not a happy camper. The carrying cage was too small and he had to scrunch down to fit. Cheeping loudly non-stop, my first thought was, "My nerves will never survive the weekend!" Our cat apparently thought the same thing. Cautiously approaching, he circled the cage. Then, he peered into the top, poised as if he expected a rattlesnake to attack. Elvis, upon seeing the cat, rushed over in a flurry, trying to peck him on the nose through the wire. Cheeping appealingly, you got the impression that he was inquiring, "Are you my mother?" Our cat on the other hand, drew back in distaste. He only had one thing on his mind and that was Spring Chicken Dinner. Scowling, our cat disappeared for the weekend.

Cheep, cheep, cheep—it was all we heard, hour after hour. I moved the cage to my studio. The boys came over to check out the weekend guest. Gazing down at the insistent little chick, they unanimously said, "he's not too cute, is he?"

"Don't you want to hold him?" I asked with disappointment.

"No way," they said, in good humor teasing me, "He never shuts up and he's ugly."

I studied Elvis's round, dark, trusting eyes. "He just needs a little time," I said, "he'll settle down." I put my hand in the cage to soothe him. He immediately rushed over and pecked me. Rubbing my hand, I said defensively as everybody chortled, "That's just his way of showing he likes you." No one wanted anything to do with him, except me.

By Saturday morning, they were all asking, *"When's that chicken going?"* I put Elvis in a bigger box and set him by me while I worked at the computer. I found his cheeping and scratching cheerful. He seemed to like the clicking sound of my keyboarding. Whenever I talked to him or called his name, he would rush over, strain his neck or cock his head to the side, trying to listen and get out of the box. I had to admit that Elvis was rather mangy looking because he had lost most of his yellow fluff and developed caramel-colored pin feathers. He had a small, pale comb on his beak, which gave him a sort of reptilian appearance. He was the most obnoxious, demanding creature I had ever met, but somehow, you had to admire his zest for life.

Monday morning, before it was time for him to return to school, I let Elvis out of the box. He was fearless, following me around wherever I went. Whenever I put my hand down, he would rush over to peck it. Nursing my hand, I asked my family if they wanted to say goodbye to Elvis. "You may never see him again," I said. Keeping their distance, they all said, "Good." Our cat came in, avoiding the cage like the plague. No one liked Elvis but me . . . but I liked him enough for everyone. Elvis is in Chicken Heaven now of course, and I grin when I think of him—pecking angels, no doubt.

I have to be reminded of how important laughter is. Rosario Castellanos tells us that, "We have to laugh, because laughter, we already know, is the first evidence of freedom." One of the most powerful passages that I've read on the true freedom of laughter was written by Ann Dawson in *A Season of Grief,* following the death of her son: ". . . I realize what a gift the ability to laugh actually is. Laughter is a song of triumph. It is a song of faith and a song of hope. It is our cry to the universe that we are undefeated by the sorrows and hardships of this life. Laughter is a hymn about overcoming obstacles and a prayer of trust that our God will comfort us and bring us joy."

God Whose Humor Infiltrates Every Corner and Creature in Creation, if you've said it once, you've said it a million times in a million ways: empowerment that rises out of laughter is of the deepest, most lasting and life-giving kind there is.

He Said

I've always admired anyone who can seemingly laugh at will. I have what many call a sense of humor but am not known for laughing out loud. Think about it, we all know someone who possesses an infectious laugh that makes us smile or laugh whenever we hear it. My high school friend, Rick was the "Ed McMahon" of our peer group and his laughter was a gift that made him popular. My sister-in-law, Gwen works at a medical clinic and one of the best antidotes she dispenses is her high-pitched cackling laughter that can be heard through the corridors of the hospital.

It has been said that people void of laughter are too serious about life. It's true that laughter connotes joy, but some of us are blessed with beautiful, encouraging smiles instead of a distinctive chuckle, cackle or guffaw. In a world of many different languages, laughter and smiles are universal; they need no interpretation. They are a God-given ability to express ourselves in the simplest form—a special gift for the purpose of spreading cheer and encouragement—our very own "release valve" if you will.

—*JPB*

She Said

Perhaps one of the hardest lessons I had to learn was being able to laugh at myself. Even at forty years of age, I was offended if anyone dared laugh at me. Wow! Did I take myself seriously! And then came that day at McDonald's. I was so excited about their latest trend, the "shaker" salad. I was wearing my new black trench coat and as my husband, son and mother–in–law began devouring their fatty cheeseburgers, I was being a bit smug about my healthy salad. I waved it vehemently as if to emphasize my smart choice. Whoosh! The salad flooded out all over my chest and lap. . . creamy ranch dressing streaming down my trench coat. My husband and son burst into laughter. Angrily, I shouted at them, "Thanks a lot for laughing! That's really just great!" I marched quickly to the bathroom and caught my scowl in the mirror. In that instant, I realized how silly it was to be so serious; how confining it was to expect perfection all the time. What a sense of relief when I gave myself permission to laugh at myself!

One of the greatest joys is sharing a chuckle with others. Raised Catholic, our family prayed to God, but also to Mary and the saints when we needed something. Losing things was a hobby of mine, so I became familiar with St. Anthony and often prayed to him until I found the searched-for item. Rarely did this kind saint let me down. . . and praying seemed to produce much more positive results than cursing. Many years later in a phone conversation I was having with Mom, I commented that I was looking for my sunglasses. "Remember to pray to St. Anthony," she clucked. "Mom," I quipped, "St. Anthony and I have been on so many searches together, I now call him *Tony.*" —*SGB*

Work Book Page

Discussion or Journal Questions

1. Talk about a time when you made a mistake you wish you had not taken so seriously and allowed yourself to laugh about. Give yourself a second chance in revisiting the memory and allow laughter this time.

2. Ed Hays suggests that humor as a response to life can become a habit through making it an *intention*. Making a commitment to humor as a life response is something we rarely think of, but it makes a lot of sense when we consider the alternatives such as anger, impatience, fear and frustration. How would you feel about viewing humor as a spiritual attitude and part of the love work you bring to the world?

Goal

To give ourselves permission to lighten up.

Task

In her book, *Everyday Epiphanies: Seeing the Sacred in Everything,* Sr. Melannie Svoboda suggests that one measure of the wholeness of our faith is our sense of humor and that we will be held accountable for everything we might have enjoyed but did not. Besides praying about obstacles and burdens that prevent us from enjoying life, we sometimes have to take action and make changes in our present lifestyle, work, career, relationships or faith practices that aren't working. Talk about a change you would like to make that could help you lighten up.

Prayer Image

An unopened, brightly wrapped present tied up in ribbons.

Affirmation Statement

I will open myself to laughter everyday, just as much as I open myself to prayer and healing life's hurts.

Part Two

Living the Journey of Faith

Now Faith is the assurance of things hoped for, the conviction of things not seen. —Hebrews 11:1

Master fear through faith—faith in the worthwhileness of life and the trustworthiness of God; faith in the meaning of our pain and our striving, the confidence that God will not cast us aside but will use each of us as a piece of priceless mosaic in the design of his universe. —*Joshua Loth*

Faith is the only link, the only connection to the source and meaning of our life. Faith is difficult. It is challenging. It is painful. It is joyful. It grows. It erodes. It grows again. It is relationship.

—*Antoinette Bosco*

But above all, faith is the opening of an inward eye, the eye of the heart, to be filled with the presence of Divine light. Ultimately faith is the only key to the universe. The final meaning of human existence, and the answers to questions on which all our happiness depends cannot be reached in any other way. —*Thomas Merton*

~ 11 ~

⟶⟶⟶ Fear, Faith and a Snake: ⟵⟵⟵
More to the Picture

. . . great is your faithfulness. "The Lord is my portion,"
says my soul, "therefore I will hope in him."
—Lamentations 3:23b, 24

ONE summer, I was busy stockpiling weeds from our flowerbed, when suddenly, I saw a black, slithering tail dart under the pile. I gasped and jerked back immediately. I am afraid of snakes, always have been, ever since I was a child and accidentally stepped on one barefoot. Now I realize, of course, that I probably frightened the snake as much as it frightened me. My snake encounter caused me to reflect on some of my past fears and what I have learned from them.

What I have discovered is that most of them were unjustified and nothing to fear at all—often a result of inexperience or lack of information. Case in point: A few years ago, I asked a friend what his greatest fear in life has been and without hesitation he spoke about his fear of taking a risk and stepping out in faith regarding his career. He stayed in a job that he strongly disliked for thirty years because he was afraid to leave what was familiar and a sure thing for the unknown. At the age of forty-nine he returned to college to study psychology and eventually found a new job that is right for him. I could see the light in his eyes and the sense of adventure he felt regarding this major life change. As he let go of regrets for not doing this sooner, he explained, ". . . I was doing my best, even though my fears and uncertainty kept me from responding to the spiritual light of encouragement that was always there."

I have found that light to be patient, consistent, revelatory and piercing, the more my faith matures and as I spiritually come of age. I am reminded of an old fear I had as a young woman exposed to new ways of thinking that were not accepted by my peers. A vibrant, young nun had begun to include the feminine nature of God in her prayer services which was considered scandalous by many. At the time, I was afraid to ask questions, be unpopular or not follow the crowd. Years later, I have come to understand what an amazing evolution each one's unique faith journey entails and I have become a voice for feminine spirituality; like the young nun, I am no longer afraid to speak up or share my heart. However, I avoid labels like *conservative* and *liberal* because of their potential to divide or segregate, believing we should all be heard.

My greatest fear has long been that of losing a child. I remember many imploring prayers for protection for my children. Somehow, I felt insulated—that if I bargained and pleaded enough with God so that I was absolutely convinced He knew how I felt— it could never happen. Then, like the lightening-fast strike of a snake, the unthinkable occurred. Our youngest son died by suicide. I felt my life was over and that along with our son's death, fear, God and faith died, too. Five years later, after suffering the deepest grief I ever hope to know, I have a whole new concept of fear and faith. Like those who find reinvention through struggle, I have found new clarity in my ministry work but this knowledge has not come without a price. The gift of this price has been the balancing and mindful vigilance of ego and comprehending how truly dependent we are upon God, others and grace when the bottom falls out. I also made a firm decision that I was not going to view life as living from one painful crisis to another but as a journey of faith that called me from one deepening experience of love to another.

I have learned that we need to converse with our fears, spend time with them and not run from them. Sue Monk Kidd writes beautifully of this in her novel, *The Secret Life of Bees,* ". . . the world was really one big bee yard, and the same rules worked fine in both places: Don't be afraid, as no life-loving bee wants to sting you. Still, don't be an idiot, wear long sleeves and long pants. Don't swat. Don't even think about swatting. If you feel angry, whistle. Anger agitates, while whistling melts a bee's temper. Act like you know what you're doing, even if you don't. Above all, send the bees love. Every little thing wants to be loved." That thought occurred to me when I was frightened of the small, harmless snake under my weed pile. Through my fear, I found myself talking to him out loud. I could see his bright eyes calmly observing me, seemingly with curiosity. For the first time in my life, I found myself feeling benevolent towards a snake, as I thought rather humorously, *there's a first time for everything,* even when that fear is over four decades old.

We all have litanies of founded and unfounded fears that are a part of our inner landscapes. Like the sight of the black, coiling tail of a snake, they fill us with dread, trepidation, withdrawal or prejudices; yet, these fears are only a small part of our life stories and history. Faith, like the head of the snake peering out of the weed pile calmly looks back at us, reminding us that there's always more to the picture than we think—that faith is more broad, deep, comforting, instructive, dependable and life-giving than we can ever imagine.

God Who Calls Us to Empowerment, when we need a bottom line, you are always there filling in the blanks.

He Said

Sitting in a cubed office mazed by hallways, waiting for my doctor, I wondered how I was going to get through this. I was stressed, not sleeping and fearing the worst possible outcome . . . prison. After spending my whole adult life serving my community and neighborhood, the federal government had indicted me on public corruption charges. "God *please* help me," I begged. Just then the door opened and I soon found hope in the attitude of my Christian doctor. "Why are you afraid if you go to jail? They will feed you. Why are you afraid if you lose your job? Another one will come along. Why are you afraid if you die? God will take care of you and your family." He insisted on not giving one minute to fear. He further explained that every minute devoted to fear was one less moment spent in joy. He also advised, "Whenever you feel fear coming on, touch your thumb and forefinger together making an "o" and whisper to yourself, "Jesus loves me."

To further prove that fear and worry did little good, he told me about a middle-aged married couple, both his patients. When the husband was diagnosed with terminal cancer, the wife fretted over life without him. How could she manage? She was becoming a basket case. A few months later, she was diagnosed with cancer and died before her husband. Our challenge, therefore, is to acknowledge our fear and begin to replace worry with prayer or praise, believing in our hearts that, "If God leads us to it, He will lead us through it." Just as he led me into my doctor's office that day.

—*JPB*

She Said

Perhaps my calling was to be an exterminator. I can hear a mouse scratch, a bat eek or a bee buzz from a mile away. Our creaky old home is a "critter's paradise." We've had squirrels in our attic, birds in our fireplace, wasp swarms in our walls, and my most feared nemesis of all, brown bats in our bedroom. I hear the flutter of their wings long before their "eeking." My innate response is a blood curdling scream as I bolt for the door, shutting it quickly behind me, and then I bravely bark instructions to my husband, whom I've abandoned to fight the flighty creature alone (he's my hero after all).

Now I know you bat lovers are disgusted with me, but I'm on a journey and I'm not yet filled with faith in this situation. My fear of bats focuses on getting rid of them. I pray that someday I will have the faith required to escort God's creature out our bedroom window, and until then I will try to learn more about saving them and less about trying to kill them. Ah . . . faith . . . a lifetime of baby steps—in this case bat steps—to react from a place of faith instead of fear.   —*SGB*

Work Book Page

Discussion or Journal Questions

1. In *The Secret Language of Signs,* Denise Linn explains that the snake has long been a symbol for healing, transformation and resurrection. "For just as the snake sheds its skin as it grows, this sign can indicate that you are shedding your old persona and beliefs to embrace a new path in life."

   Talk about your faith journey through the years. Are there specific instances when you felt as if you had shed your skin and found yourself and your faith changed and renewed?

2. In thinking about your future and the fears or reservations you have known, what is a "beneath-the-surface" fear that you would like to leave behind? Spend some time meditating on the possibility of hidden faith that resides within your experiences waiting to reveal itself and rise to the occasion.

Goal

To learn not to make narrow, surface judgments as we remember that there are hidden dimensions to life and faith that we don't begin to comprehend with our limited human vision.

Task

By framing our life experiences as an unfolding journey of adventure, we learn to be less intimidated by the future. What excites you? What new thing would you like to try? What old interest or passion might you like to revisit and explore? Often, in exploring hidden or deeply rooted fears, we simultaneously find the gift of forgotten or unacknowledged talents being called into a new service or phase. What comes to mind?

Prayer Image

An iceberg.

Affirmation Statement

Respecting human frailty and not having walked in anyone's shoes but my own, I will not make narrow, unfair or condescending surface judgments about the fears of others.

—❋ The Violins of Autumn: ❋— Faith Everlasting

As long as the earth endures, seedtime and harvest, cold and heat, summer and winter, day and night, shall not cease. —Genesis 8:22

WHEN the wind sweeps through the trees and the leaves drift down in the fall, sometimes I remember my mother's voice calling, *"Come hommmme,"* when it was time for supper and I was off playing somewhere on the farm.

I remember those autumns of my girlhood, when idyllic summer passed into autumn, bringing a heightened sense of something completed. The trees in the apple orchard, like our old gray mother cat when pregnant, drooped with the weight of full term, juicy red apples. The pasture grass lay long and cured to the color of wheat, which in contrast to the brilliant blue sky was breathtaking. The barn, newly painted a rich, blood-red with white trim sported new blue shingles, ready for a batch of baby Angus calves which were due any day. I remember my dad whistling in the barn as he spread fragrant, shiny, yellow straw for them.

Sounds seemed to carry on the wind as Old Time and Big Band music drifted from the kitchen radio and in my memory I could hear Mom clattering pots and pans as she put supper on the table. Later, after the dishes were done, darkness fell like God pulling a shade, while the sound of mourning doves could be heard from the distant grove where I had my tree house. Their alluring song blended into a whole host of sounds as crickets started up and frogs could be heard croaking from the slough. A cow mooing content-edly from the barnyard added to the cadence while a million stars came out.

I remember the chickens that went to roost for the night in the branches of the trees, their heads tucked under their wings while fireflies flickered about. Bats darted here and there eating bugs and hummingbird moths flitted softly among the velvet petals of my mother's petunias, dimly visible by the yard light. After playing bat and ball with my sister, I remember going out to the pasture to visit Polly, our old work horse and my best friend, her worn leather hal-ter jingling as she nudged my shoulder. I would give her a hearty scratching on her shoulders, neck and between the ears as I declared, "Best horse God ever made," watching as a cloud passed over the moon, momentarily plunging the pasture and world into darkness.

The wind brushed across my damp face, ruffling my bangs and the leaves rustled in the branches of a nearby Box Elder tree, mak-ing a rattling sound. I remember Polly raising her head with a jerk, her mouth half-full of grass, listening to the squeak-squish, squeak-squish sound of my tennis shoes on the grass soggy with dew. It was the kind of night when every sound echoed musically across the farm, and I heard Mom call, *"Time for beddddd"* from the porch. I cupped my hands to my mouth and called back, *"Beeeee right there. . . "* as the wind swept through the trees yet again and more leaves scuttled to my feet.

Paul Verlaine once wrote, "The long sobs/of the violins/of autumn/pierce my heart" and so it is each year that we are remind-ed that the earth prepares for winter and things pass away, only to be reborn in the spring. The beauty of experiencing this transition of seasons defies words; to witness it a privilege beyond comparison. Before the winter winds that blast the land, we gather autumn to our breasts, its golden, poignant days and memories like a cloak wrapping itself around us. "This, too shall pass," we say, as we reflect upon the present days. They become all the more precious because we know they are fleeting. Faith, however, hovers closer, ever present in the seasonal rites of passage that take place upon the land, within our world and within our prayers. Like our mother's voices echoing *"Come hommmme"* down the years, faith and autumn call us home to our hearts and the things we can be sure of—reminding us, as Helen Keller once wrote, "What we once enjoyed and deeply loved we can never lose, for all that we love deeply becomes a part of us."

> *Prayer: God of Falling Leaves and Autumn Faith, thank you for ceaselessly calling us home to faith that never dies.*

He Said

My Dad often remarked that the best thing about living in Minnesota was the change of seasons. I agreed—especially about autumn. We buzzed around our garage like frenzied bees, cleaning it out as we searched for items to donate to our church's fall festival. We also had to rake leaves, mow and fertilize the lawn a final time, pull flowers, put the air conditioner away and bring plants inside.

But despite the beauty of nature's changing colors, there was one color that was synonymous with fall and colder temperatures . . . a small beady orange light draped over the headboard of my bed. As if it were yesterday, I can remember running up the stairs to the bedroom I shared with my twin brother. The room would be dark, but that little orange light glowed. "She did it!" I'd exclaim, reveling in the fact that Mom had gone into the attic, brought out our electric blankets and winterized our bed, turning on the control panel early so the bed would be toasty warm. It was heavenly to snuggle in and have only my nose touching the icy air outside my cozy cave. Whenever I think of that warm blanket, I begin to yawn, taking me back to the days of footed pajamas, warm milk before bed and a complete feeling of safety. . . much like the hug of God.

—*JPB*

She Said

In October 2001, we were arguing before church again. "But I don't want to go to *that* church" I pined, "I need something more." My husband loved his traditional boyhood church because it was known and comfortable, but after 9/11, I was searching for a place that felt emotionally real. Acquiescing, he suggested trying a church he'd been receiving a bulletin from all summer. The contrast was amazing. When we arrived, complete strangers greeted and welcomed us. Looking ahead, the full rock-hewn wall was bare save a large cross with Jesus on it, so unlike the ornate angels, pillars and porcelain statutes of our other church.

Three minutes into the service, Father Greg challenged us to mingle about the church and meet three people we didn't know— a stark contrast to the individual space we guarded like sentinels at our other church. A while later his homily discussed personal, heart-wrenching pain as he discussed losing his mother when he was age 10, and losing his sister Patty Jo when she was only 9 and he was 19 and then another sister to the very disease he was fighting: cystic fibrosis. During the Eucharist, beautiful choral music flowed over me and I could not help but weep slow, steady, therapeutic tears. I was home. I felt like the prodigal daughter. From what I saw, heard and read that day, I experienced the *agape* love of God and shared it with others there . . . black, white, brown, gay, man, woman, ill, well, rich, poor, liberal, conservative, centrist. "Home" is the freedom to be yourself and to be wholly accepted.

—*SGB*

Work Book Page

Discussion or Journal Questions

1. Recount a beautiful Homecoming memory that is a touch-stone of faith and of feeling loved, secure and empowered following a time of feeling lost. Amplify the memory through meditation as you remember the sounds, smells, sights and feelings surrounding the memory. Write it down and put it in your Bible or a special book so that you can return to it and share it with others. Consider having the remembrance framed and hung in your office, above a home altar or any place that feels special to you. Perhaps you might like to even print out copies to include in your Christmas cards.

2. Lou Gehrig was not only a great baseball legend who along with Babe Ruth played for the New York Yankees, his name is synonymous with the disease that took his life, ALS (Amyotrophic Lateral Sclerosis) known as Lou Gehrig's Disease. He is also known for giving one of the most famous speeches ever made in baseball history at Yankee Stadium on July 4, 1939, when he said farewell to the love of his life—baseball, and all his friends, family and devoted fans. Even in the face of disability and impending death, he eulogized himself as "the luckiest man on the face of the earth." Why? Because he had lived passionately at home with his soul. If someone asked what impassions you, what would you say?

Goal

To discover, acknowledge, embrace and trust that which we can spiritually *be sure of.*

Task

When many inner voices and outer demands are clamoring for attention, our task is to develop the ability to *respond* to that knowing whisper that says, "Come home to yourself."

Talk about the books, scripture verses and well-known people who inspire you to personally respond to the call of inner deepening in your life.

Prayer Image

A homing pigeon.

Affirmation Statement

When I come home to my heart of hearts, I return again and again to a living, transforming, eternal faith that transcends all seasons, sorrows and troubles I face.

~ 13 ~

— What Our Hearts Become: — The Greatest Bond

If we live by the spirit, let us also be guided by the spirit.
—Galatians 5:25

IN my dictionary, the word *compassion*, described as *a sympathy with the suffering of others*, is preceded by the word *compass*, defined as *an instrument for showing direction*. The link and bond between these two words struck me as profound, following recent conversations. Someone had asked me, after hearing my story of having lost a child to suicide, "Do you find that people avoid you?" I wrote back: "The answer has two parts and the first is yes. My family and I did find that folks who prefer only surface conversations did avoid us at first. We can certainly understand this; some people are uncomfortable with the tragedy we have known, they simply don't know what to say to us. . . and we remind them of the proverbial "bad thing that can happen to good people." Secondly, we found that because of what we have experienced, people who are struggling with fear and troubles are drawn to us. They seem to sense our receptivity and empathy to the wounds of others. Because of my outreach work, I hear from people I don't know—such as a wonderful woman who asked how to comfort her best friend who had lost a child in a tragic accident. This woman (whom I will call China) was also traumatized herself because she was the one who had to call her friend and tell her that her child had died. In my letter to this beautiful woman, I wrote:

"China, my heart goes out to you and your friend. Please be comfortable with the fact that your friend may not be able to comprehend the language of comfort for a time. She is going to keep reliving the actual incident of how her child died, trying to wrap her mind around what happened and why. She may well have panic attacks, which can feel like jolts of electricity raging through her body. She won't be able to sleep and when she does, she will sleep the numbed sleep of the dead or have dreams filled with remembered nightmares. Her faith may plummet or be her rock to cling to—probably both.

"She will become a completely re-invented person. The fierce insanity of grief will mark much of the first year of her loss. By the second year, you will be able to see the progress she is making, as she learns that her beloved child would want her to be happy and that she needs to let go so that love can flow and fill the void. You will hear the sound of her laughter again and see that it is possible for passion and purpose to rise out of the greatest heartache a person can know—but know also that she will be forever altered and marked by her grief, as Mary was when Jesus died.

"The most important lesson she will learn is that a person can't make a journey like this alone. God will bring friends like you and other gift persons into her life to listen and bring care. It is to you, China— for your heart—that I tell you to take courage and confidence; your friend can and will survive this. The eternal love of her child will carry her, she will be embraced . . . but the journey will be brutal for a time. This can't be changed, but a tenderness comes, a power for living she never knew she had will emerge . . . and a knowing and peace that defies all human understanding will come to her, *if she is open to it and relies on faith.* As Ann Dawson writes in *A Season of Grief,* 'I eventually came to know the meaning of a 'holy darkness,' a time when pain and sorrow is all-engulf-ing and we no longer have even the strength to struggle against the dark. When we are so worn out and exhausted that we allow the darkness to swallow us up—that holy darkness is when we experi-ence God.' "

Let your own hurting heart float; there is nothing else that can be done at this time for the newly bereaved and nothing required—except this surrender into the love of God and each other. When your friend is ready, present her with a gold compass . . . because that is what her heart will become, *a living compass,* a symbol which she alone will learn to define. Her inner heart will direct her to the avenues of faith and comfort that she needs. In time, if she says yes, compassion will make a home in her . . . and she will become a compass for others who are wounded and have lost the way.

As Sam Keen says so well in *Hymns to an Unknown God,* "In the spiritual journey, the compass unfailingly points toward compas-sion. This spiritual compass is the equivalent of the satellite Ground Position System that pilots and ship captains use to dis-cover their exact location. Inscribe this single word on your heart—'compassion.' Whenever you are confused, keep heading in the direction that leads toward deepening your love and care for all liv-ing beings, including yourself, and you will never stray far from the path to fulfillment."

God, Our Living Compass and Guide in Every Way,
help us to remember that there is no greater bond or hope
for the world than compassion and entering one anoth-
er's suffering.

He Said

Compassion is a passion for helping others. I have always wondered why some people are more loving and caring than others. For example, in an inner city neighborhood, why do only 1% of the residents choose to become active in seeking improvement? Why will one person stop and help a desperate senior with car problems, but another person drive by, seemingly indifferent and cold? In the same vein why does one politician speak passionately about finding ways to help the downtrodden while another politician promotes financial cuts in aid to the poor? Did God give a compassionate heart to some and not others?

Frankly, I've come to the conclusion that not enough people are willing to give compassion an honest try. They fulfill their family obligations, but not much more. Many years ago, our Catholic School needed a Little League coach. I volunteered, thinking it would entail babysitting young boys. Instead, it was a challenging, maturing, and rewarding experience. I connected with the thinking of a younger generation and developed a rapport that still exists today. My former players, now grown adults, still call me "coach" when we see each other. What an honor it is to be a mentor to a child and make a difference in their lives. God calls us to help each other by using the talents we possess and *everyone* has a talent. Possessing compassion is in and of itself a talent, but it is useless unless it is shared.

—*JPB*

She Said

Our family's favorite ritual is to gather during the holidays and watch Frank Capra's classic film, *It's a Wonderful Life*. George Bailey is given the unique opportunity to see how different life in the town of Bedford Falls would have been if he had never been born. Through George Bailey's kindness and compassion he improved the lives of many. In the end, his friends gather to get him out of his financial predicament. George realizes that a truly rich man is one with family and friends (and faith, might I add).

Although I never particularly cared about the politics of politics, I always appreciated the good my husband could do in his role as a public servant. He and his colleagues were able to add to our city's infrastructure with schools, housing, libraries and park buildings. I kid him and tell him he is like "George Bailey." But the things for which I am most proud of him will never make the annals of history: helping an out-of-work friend fill out a job application; treating city staff with respect and courtesy and giving them credit for their hard work; visiting a little girl at the hospital who was attacked by a pit bull, and going to funerals of his constituents who he came to regard as part of his extended family. In my estimation, the mark of a great person is how much kindness they have shared with others—so that they, too, can join in the refrain, "IT'S A WONDERFUL LIFE!"   —*SGB*

Work Book Page

Discussion and Journal Questions

1. The image of Mary embracing the crucified body of Christ in
    her lap is one of the most powerful and wrenching portrayals of
    bonded compassion known to the world. In her beautiful book,
    Your Sorrow is My Sorrow, Joyce Rupp writes, "We can under-
    stand the *Pieta* as a posture of our heart when we are caught in
    the grips of goodbye or when we are tending to others who are
    suffering grievously. . . . Mary is everyone filled with anguish
    and sorrow who has held what has died in their life and won-
    dered why it happened." Joyce invites us to understand what it
    means to be a living *Pieta*.

    Talk about a time when something bad happened to you or
    someone else and there was nothing you could say or do to
    remedy or change the tragedy. How does the image of the *Pieta*
    alter the sense of hopelessness and helplessness?

2. Talk about what drains you and prevents you from envisioning
    the fullness of faith which Mary epitomizes. If Mary were to
    offer you consolation or thoughts of wisdom, what do you think
    she would say? What correlation do you see between being a liv-
    ing compass and a living *Pieta?*

Goal

To better understand what it means to spiritually hold pain for
others and ourselves.

Task

When Mary embraced her crucified son, besides the pain, she
was also embracing all the laughter, hopes, dreams, faith, memories
and devotion. Her lap did not hold only sorrow but the legacy her
son left for the whole world. Mary did not hold sorrow in her lap
forever, but rather joy and glory.

Have you been holding a sorrow too long that needs to be
embraced by faith and transformed into resurrected hope and
empowered living?

Prayer Image

A loving parent rocking a hurt child.

Affirmation Statement

The greatest bond and the greatest guiding force both arise out
of one word: compassion.

14

─── A Living Compass: ───
Giving Witness

. . . be a true and faithful witness . . .   —Jeremiah 42:5

HOLIDAYS are especially tough for people who are grieving. The emptiness and "presence of absence" of the missing loved one is never more apparent, painful or poignant. As
one mother said, "You get used to it. . . " but happiness is never
the same. There is an important lesson to be learned here; as
Adolfo Quezada explains in his important book *Rising From the
Ashes,* "being happy is not the same as being joyful. Joy is a consequence of our faith, joy emanates from God . . . happiness
comes and goes with the wind of circumstance." For the
bereaved, that promise of faith and joy often brings memories
and symbols that give one courage, direction and the comfort
needed to go on. This happened for me as I faced the third
Christmas without our son. I wrote:

"Dusk has fallen, but it is so white and luminous from the
snowstorm you can still see uptown in our village from the porch.
The air seems foggy or like it is filled with static electricity, the
sound reminiscent of a deep, faraway ocean roaring in the woods.
The creaking tree trunks appear coal black in contrast to the
whiteness, their armpits and undersides flocked from storm-driven
snow. Like black and white winter garter snakes, the Cork Screw
Willow branches entwine and coil in the wind.

"The snow has drifted across the yards, houses, stalled cars and
thorny shrubbery, blurring boundaries while the heavily-laden

branches of the giant evergreen trees droop with the weight. Their limbs seem alive in the storm, lifting here and there and seeming to whisper a language that only the wild creatures know. The street lights blink on, one by one, glowing dully like hazy, bronze-colored portals or beacons into another world. And thus it comes, the arrival of our first snowstorm of the year—beautiful beyond words—and sometimes fierce, like life.

"Closing the door on the scene and gathering the neck of my cardigan tighter, I stand warming my outstretched hands before our fireplace. Well acquainted with portals of the heart, I slip easily into another time and place: It is a perfect night, our village streets deserted, the breeze faint and cool. Mic and I are taking a moonlight bike ride, our traditional farewell to summer. Grinning, Mic describes it perfectly as a giant flashlight in the sky. The moon dominates, casting white patches on the road through the leafy branches. Our bike tires crunch loudly on the loose gravel and the sound seems intrusive in the otherwise absence of sound. 'Shhh,' we say, as we pass the darkened houses. It seems we're the only ones awake.

"We pedal slowly, breathing deeply and not talking. The cornfield looms dark and dense, a presence in the night you can feel. Suddenly, our tires hit the main street pavement and we glide along silently now, in sync with the night energy. All the while, we keep our faces upturned toward the moon, which like a compass, seems to guide us. There is not a dog or cat in sight and not even any frogs croaking. We bike to our destination—the stop sign bordering the highway—and turning around, coast back down to the pop machine. Four quarters later find Mic and I perching companionably on the picnic table in the gazebo nestled in the park— sentries giving witness to the change of seasons."

The memory fades and I return to the present, a sentry now to the coming of the third Christmas following the death of our son. My heart has become a living compass that guides me to beacons of faith that comfort. Along with many others, I give witness to the endurance and resilience of the human spirit and while the wise men followed a star to Bethlehem, in my mind I envision the star as a giant flashlight that shines through eternal portals of love.

> *Christmas God of Gifts of the Heart, to become a living compass is the most profound gift that happens to us . . . completely and utterly beyond words.*

He Said

As we entered church one Sunday morning, our pastor distributed baseball-sized rocks to everyone. He instructed us to hold the rock during mass. Our pastor's homily focused on life on Earth and the fact that we as humans are merely passing through; the rock was here long before us and would remain long after us. He encouraged us to take the rock with us, look at it when we felt overwhelmed or got off track. As Christians, the Bible directs us to fill our hearts with joy, knowing that Jesus' death covered our sins, and opened the gateway to everlasting life. Though we will experience trials and pain on earth, they are momentary in the scheme of eternal life. I was deeply moved by the sermon and took the rock to my office, placing it on the corner of my desk next to the picture of my family.

A few days later I was working late in my office, a million chores to do and thinking about how much I could get done if I stayed

and worked a few more hours. As I scanned my desk for a particular file, my eye caught the rock and the adjacent picture of my
family. I heard my pastor's words, "We are only passing through.
We are only here for a short while." A few seconds later, I shut off
the lights and go home to the family God has blessed me with, cog-
nizant that nourishing relationship with my family is another
important job God asks of me.   *—JPB*

She Said

I was ambivalent about attending my 25th class reunion. After
all, my husband was fighting a legal battle and his picture was making the local nightly news consistently. "Could I, the ex-home-
coming queen, have fallen so far from grace and still show her face
at the ball?" Not really taking my "royal-ship" all that seriously, I
signed up to go, invited my husband, and prayed for inner
strength. The first person to hug and welcome me at the Wabasso
Community Center that evening was Laurie, a classmate of mine,
who had lost her 21-year-old son in a freak auto accident six
months earlier. Talk was a little stilted at first, but soon I was cele-
brating with a classmate who had triumphed over a bout with alco-
holism, commiserating with another who had just been diagnosed
with multiple sclerosis, and was exchanging stories of raising children with long-ago friends. After 25 years, we were able to accept
life for what it was—good and bad, ugly and beautiful.

As I thumbed through the book of my classmates' reflections I
smiled at the one I had chosen. It was not the motto that I lived
life by for 24 years, Stephen De Grellet's saying that if there be any
kindness I can show, or any good thing I can do, let me do it now
for I shall not pass this way again. Instead it was the one simple
phrase I had taken to heart this past year, the excerpt that Jesus

gave us in the Our Father, "give us this day our daily bread." Only now during our hardship, did I understand the significance of this verse, that God provides us with *daily* bread because that is all we need, and getting through one day at a time was all that was expected. Tomorrow would carry its own worries, but God would provide and we would survive . . . together . . . one day at a time.

—*SGB*

Work Book Page

Discussion and Journal Questions

1. When snow falls, the world as we knew it is transformed and blanketed in pristine newness, completely altered. What life experiences have completely altered your world? Talk about a time when you found renewal of joy and hope through faith.

2. To make a covenant is to make a promise or commitment. Have you ever thought about making a promise or renewing one to be a witness for goodness, justice, love, forgiveness and God? If you would like to do so, write it out, sign it and share it with someone to give witness to your resolve.

Goal

To explore what it means to be a witness of faith regarding the differences between earthly happiness and spiritual joy.

Task

To be clothed with power from on high reveals the greatest key to witnessing: we do not do it alone, but rather with God's healing presence cloaking our human vulnerabilities, hurts and fear. Sometimes when we live without mindfulness and make poor choices, we unconsciously become witnesses of gloom, materialism, doubt or unhealthy life styles.

Ask someone you trust how they honestly perceive you as a witness to joyful living. Listen thoughtfully and courageously—and then positively use the information to make specific changes.

Prayer Image

The great cloud of witnesses found in Hebrews 12:1.

Affirmation Statement

How I live my life and respond to life's challenges gives witness to the greatest hope that can only be found through authentic example.

15

The Optimist Challenge: A Choice Offered

It is I, Jesus, who sent my angel to you . . .
—Revelation 22:16

ONE year, I decided to actively engage in optimism for the holidays and new year. Having known a lot of challenges and tragedy, I decided that I wanted to make some changes in how I coped with daily life, especially keeping things in perspective.

In his powerful book, *The Optimistic Child* by Martin E.P. Seligman, Ph.D., the point is made that optimism can be a psychologically learned trait. He explains that strong emotions exist for a purpose because they galvanize you into action to change yourself or your world and that "they are not mere inconveniences but of crucial use in that each bears a message." Spiritually, as I explored just what that meant, it proved to be quite an adventure that affirmed my progress and hope. Through my studies I learned that those who are hopeful are better equipped to withstand hardship and thus endure for the long haul—even though they experience just as many challenges as anyone else. In one of the most beautiful passages in Paul Rogat Loeb's *Soul of a Citizen*, he links hope, optimism and faith: "The novelist David Bradley describes this faith as a fundamental trust that 'somewhere, never mind exactly where, something good and right and fair is happening which someday, never mind exactly when, will make itself apparent; that in some distant constellation a star has flamed up to unaccustomed brilliance, and what we must do is wait for the arrival of the light. Because this light is always and everywhere immanent, ready to reveal itself, our religious traditions remind us that we're never completely alone and forsaken.' "

A poignant example of this was revealed in two dreams my husband had, several years apart. When our son died, he had a terrible nightmare of a wall of scissors. This dream portrayed the terror he felt and the fact that he felt cut off from consolation and unable to move forward because he was blocked by a wall of what seemed like insurmountable grief. Much later, he dreamt again about the walls of scissors—but this time, it was in a maze-like tunnel and he was being borne swiftly through it within the wings of a mighty angel that exuded light, purpose and splendor. The appearance of the angel in the dream was—as Bradley wrote—a star flaming up, ushering in a new era of hope, optimism and service, which clearly became a calling in his life. As Jerry learned in his Death, Dying and Bereavement class, in psychological terms especially in near death experience, the "wall" is noted as the scientific ending of life biologically, while the "tunnel" is seen as continuation. When it is time to move forward, we should not wait for great strength before setting out because inertia will only weaken us. Rather, we are to walk toward the light one step at a time, whereupon we will find our endurance doubled.

Dr. Seligman says that there are only two tactics available to us when something bad happens. We can stay in the situation and act, trying to terminate the emotion by changing the situation, or we can give up and leave the situation. The first is called mastery and the second, learned helplessness. Optimism is not chanting happy thoughts, blaming others or avoiding sadness or anger and it is not a cure-all. Rather, we should view spiritual optimism not only as a powerful tool, but as a sacred resilience that is co-created in us through the processing of life's heartaches.

> *GodWho Directs Our Heavenly Helpers, remind us that optimism is an angelic momentum that guides all humans beyond restrictive walls of sorrow, injustice and helplessness to passageways of hope, recovery and service.*

He Said

We were born of the same parents, raised in the same house, attended the same Catholic school, but that glass he saw as half full was always half empty in my view. My older brother Leonard possessed an uncanny talent for optimism—seeing the good side in every situation. For example, when we bought older homes, he considered an electrical problem as "an opportunity to do some needed updating," whereas I fretted about the cost, inconvenience and my lack of expertise. As years passed, when I said we were getting older, he said we were maturing. When we took up exercise, I called it jogging; he called it running. We entered our first five-mile benefit run. I agonized at the three-mile mark moaning "two more miles to go?" He rejoiced that three miles were already behind us. When we decided to learn golf and laughed at our many swings and misses, I went home thinking I'd never learn the game; he stopped by the library on the way home to pick up a book on golf thinking he wasn't missing the ball by much.

When my optimism has wavered, faith has taken control for me. I know God has already written His plan for me and this gives me the foundation of hope. Still, I work hard at practicing optimism and have made progress. Reading scripture daily is the most important thing I do. This instills in me the desire to be positive since God is in control and to accept things as they are with the secure knowledge that God will never abandon me and will always love me. God has filled my glass to the brim. Cheers!   —*JBP*

She Said

I attribute my positive attitude to my mother. She has a patient, calming, caring presence and experiences life in the moment. Despite being raised with seven siblings in a very small home, space and love were not lacking. My mother greeted each day with a good sense of humor, encouraging us to "do the best we could" and letting us define what that best was.

Empathizing with me about a difficult time I was experiencing, she relayed a harrowing time in her life: Giving birth to my sister Lynn in July of 1958, she realized something was very wrong when in April my sister constantly whined and slept poorly. After many doctor visits, a specialist diagnosed neuroblastoma, a cancerous tumor, on baby Lynn's adrenal gland. Concurrently, my mom was pregnant with me and due to complications in the pregnancy she was banned from any lifting or riding in a car. My dad drove 120 miles to "the cities' " University Hospital to be with baby Lynn. It was excruciating for my Mom to participate at a distance... unable to comfort Lynn, missing her first birthday on July 20 and not present for the surgery on July 23. Many prayers later, miracles occurred. Lynn survived and thrived after many doses of Vitamin B12. And I arrived a premie at 4$^{1}/_{2}$ pounds the end of September and have been kicking and screaming ever since.   —*SGB*

Work Book Page

1. In *Gold in Your Memories,* Macrina Wiederkehr says that sometimes, ". . . when people are drawn into working with memories these days, there is an excessive concentration on the
   painful memories." She teaches that while it is necessary to
   receive, accept and integrate troubling memories and experiences into our lives so that healing can take place, she suggests
   that our joyful memories are often overlooked.

   Spend some time thinking about joyful memories you may have
   forgotten. At random and in no particular order, write down
   five happy memories that come to mind and share them with
   someone.

2. Macrina teaches that our memories come to us all mixed up,
   that it is quite possible to be happy and sad all in the same
   moment—and that the daily dyings and risings in our own life
   experiences connect us to the death and resurrection of Jesus.
   Talk about a Paschal moment you experienced by recalling
   something good or heroic in someone else or yourself that was
   woven into the fabric of a dark time or bad experience in your
   life.

Goal

To learn to integrate painful experiences into a framework that
moves beyond singular negativity to a complementary vision that
seeks and embraces beauty, comfort, faith, support of others, our
own courage and meaningful living.

Task

In the well-known story *A Christmas Carol* by Charles Dickens,
hidden beneath the robe of the Ghost of Christmas Past are the

needy children of Humanity, Want and Ignorance. It has occurred to me that beneath our secular robes of painful experiences, Negativity and Hopelessness would reside. If I were to present a visitation story of three ghosts or angels to appear that would teach us to open our hearts to the true spirit of Optimism, I would name them Peace, Passion and Purpose.

Imagine that you are writing a play about your painful experiences. By what names would you entitle the needy children beneath your robes? By what names would you call the three ghosts who would transform your hope and thereby usher in a new era of empowerment? How would your play unfold? What would the setting be? How would it end?

Prayer Image

A glass half full.

Affirmation Statement

The first active step beyond helplessness always begins with spiritual optimism.

~ 16 ~

➤ Exodus to the Light: ➤
Instinctive Faith

Draw near to God and he will draw near to you.

—James 4:8

NATURE is our world and we have an intuitive sense to learn of and from it. I had a very dramatic experience of this when our village was invaded by Asian beetles that were introduced to devour the aphids that were wiping out crops. I had stepped outdoors to appreciate one of the last warm days of the season before winter set in. However, within seconds, flying insects tangled in my hair and crawled in my ears and down the neck of my shirt. Flailing at them, I dashed into the house as literally thousands of them encrusted the front of our house like it was a giant beehive—only these were not bees—they were beetles that resembled orange and black lady bugs. They infiltrated every crack or crevice and reminded me of a biblical pestilence. Their invasion was the talk of the town.

That night, while reading in my sitting room, I began to hear a popping, rustling sound overhead. I looked up and right above me, the ceiling was writhing with well over a hundred of the beetles, drawn to the light of my reading lamp. We had antique, tin-sculpted ceilings, which have a lot of unsealed crevices and the bugs were getting in through the attic. Shocked, I flew off the daybed, wondering what to do. Then, I got an idea. I snapped off the light, plunging the room into darkness and put the light on in an adjoining closet. Within seconds, it was as if a command was issued and the beetles swarmed *en masse* across the ceiling as a community, like the exodus out of Egypt. They gathered on the walls of the closet where I could sweep them down into a dust pan and empty them outside. I'd never witnessed such a dramatic, immediate response to the lure of light—it was a wonder to me!

For several days, the experience stayed with me as I thought of the compelling power of light. I thought about what it is like to spiritually journey out of darkness into the light of optimism, hope and healing. I realized that beyond our hardships, sorrows and challenges, we are all on an exodus to the light. From deep within the intricate, beautiful and complex webs we weave in our hearts, we are instinctively drawn to the illuminating consolation of prayer, faith and communion with God. It draws us on the darkest night, when we have lost our way. Always present, always planted within our being, always a reality—love draws us home to God's heart and our true selves as surely as beetles are drawn to light.

The Bible is infused with stories of lost souls straying from the love and light of God by becoming infatuated and lured by worldly pleasures, power, lust and jealousy. God always lets them go but never stops calling them back home to their first love. They have the freedom to go but more importantly, the freedom to come back to the light is always there. We are in good company: Adam and Eve, Cain, the people of Noah's day, the builders of the Tower of Babel, Lot's wife, Jacob who impersonated his brother Esau, Joseph's brothers, the Israelites and Aaron who made the golden calf idol, King David, Job and Jonah, to name a few. As it was prophesied in scriptures of old, *the people who walked in darkness have seen a great light,* who, as introduced in the New Testament, is Christ the Lord, the Light of the World. Through him, light takes on a whole new meaning. It is in the glow of radiant light that the

Angel Gabriel appears to Mary; light fills the sky as an angel announces to the shepherds, "for today, in the city of David, a Saviour has been born to you . . . " Jesus Himself instructs us in Matthew 5:15, "No one after lighting a lamp puts it under the bushel basket but on the lampstand, and it gives light to all in the house. In the same way, let your light shine before others . . . "

Through all the hard times of my life, I have had dreams of being a student. In dream after dream, there I'd be in a classroom, earnestly studying and trying to understand the dynamics of my challenges and experiences. Suddenly, after years of being the student, for the first time ever, I had a vivid dream that I had become the teacher of the class. When I woke up, I was filled with joy! My dream portrayed the power and glory of choice at its deepest level. Instead of saying no to learning from my life stories, I said yes. . . and in light of that choice, as it does for all who make the same decision, the pupil becomes the teacher. Light calls to light.

> *God Who Is Our Impulse for Meaningful Living, may we always remember that while our ever-present spiritual instincts beckon us to the light and love of God, it is always our choice how or if we respond.*

He Said

I always believed in Him, I just didn't know Him. That's the way I described my relationship with Christ before my bubbly, vibrant, born-again niece convinced me to attend one of her bible study classes. Until then, I was what one might call a tire-kicker. Sure, I knew there was more. I wanted to see the light but wasn't God going to come to me, knock on my door? You know like the Publisher's Clearinghouse Sweepstakes announcer who brings good tidings of your new millionaire status! Or in this case the hundred kilowatt spiritual winner!

Gaining spiritual maturity through this bible study taught me otherwise. The more I seek Him, the more He comes to me. I now realize that God is made happy by people seeking Him. He is not someone you should call on only when you are in need. He is not an order-taker. He is a loving, open God who wants us to need Him, to thank Him, to love Him and to praise Him. My previous world was clouded with foggy thinking. This new awareness has illuminated my outlook. Now, each day I make a list under the title "Blessings of the Day" and record the good things that happen to me large and small. I realize that God has been hearing me and responding in a variety of ways. It is my job to see these nuances and surrender control to Him.　　　　　　　—*JPB*

She Said

Catching my eye, I watch the searchlights crisscrossing our night city sky, and wonder what new club is opening or what theater production is beckoning the curious to come. I imagine the star of Bethlehem much like that, the bright silver star piercing through an indigo velvet sky, coaxing weary travelers to continue their journey.

On my lifelong quest for meaning, I witness Christ's birth, death and resurrection as significant and sacred. Needing a concrete symbol, I asked my friend who works with silver to put this idea in symbolic form: the eight-pronged star of Bethlehem as the backdrop depicting birth, a smaller cross on top of that depicting Christ's death, and a smaller symbol (of two squares juxtaposed so they overlap creating an 8-point star) for "rebirth" for the resurrection on top. The layers alternate light, darkness, light, for we cannot have one without the other—they define each other's essence, just as Christ's light exposes, eclipses and triumphs over darkness. Although I never experienced an earth-shattering "born again" moment like my friends describe, I do understand the slow, maturing "rebirth" that I'm experiencing every day as I grow closer to Christ and acknowledge He is my light and salvation.

—*SGB*

Work Book Page

Discussion or Journal Questions

1. Would you describe your personal faith as shining from a lampstand, hidden under a bushel basket or both? Offer examples and reflections that further describe your answer.

2. Three weeks before Christmas 2003, my Aunt Eleanore and Uncle Ormund sent me eight narcissus bulbs. With my cat Tubby eagerly watching, I planted the little dead bulbs in the provided dirt in a deep blue crystal bowl. As white, fragrant flowers began to bloom, I reflected on the challenging year I had just experienced. For my New Year's Resolution I resolved to make sure that I kept my life watered and lit from spiritual resources that I instinctively knew would encourage endurance, resilience and trust.

Plant a bulb or seed, water it and give it light, and see what happens. If you were to make specific, realistic new resolutions or goals that would help you walk closer to the light, what would they be? Make a list and put it someplace where you will see it often.

Goal

To learn to trust and rely more deeply on spiritual instincts and to consciously become more mindful in making choices that reflect this way of living through faith.

Task

In your Bible, look up and highlight the following verses on light from the Psalms. Allow memories, lessons, images, mistakes and renewed resolutions to rise through the verses as they speak to you personally regarding your own life: Psalms 27:1, 37:6, 43:3, 49:19, 97:11, 119:105, 119:130, 139:12.

Prayer Image

The Israelites entering the Promised Land.

Affirmation Statement

Spiritual intuition and instinct will always draw me out of the darkness and isolation of my struggles to the empowerment of light and the companionship of like-minded soulmates and friends.

~ 17 ~

⚒ Reservoirs of Faith: ⚒
Living Waters

. . . out of the believers heart shall flow rivers of living water. —John 7:38b

I HAVE many memories of how precious water is. When I was a child, my earliest memory is of Mom heating water in a teakettle on the stove for our bath water. We had a round, galvanized steel tub on the kitchen floor and she would fill it with warm, soapy water until it was full. My sisters and I would then have our ritual Saturday night bath, and I fondly recall suds all over Mom and the linoleum and the joy of those early baths.

We did not have indoor running water yet and Mom had to carry in all the water we used, which was a lot of work for her. For drinking, we had a water pail on our counter with a dipper and Mom would keep it filled by drawing icy cold water from an iron hand pump down by the barn next to our cow tank. I remember one time, Dad rigged up a shower for himself behind our house from a hose that ran into a small oval water tank. We thought Dad was funny and innovative, and that we were so modern to have a shower under our apple tree. I also remember how my parents had a small cistern well dug by our house that could catch all the rainwater that ran off our roof, so we could have soft water for washing clothes. Not a drop was wasted and if there was no rain, the cistern would be empty.

We had a creek that meandered through our pasture and I spent many happy hours lying on my stomach on our old wooden field bridge, mesmerized by all the fish, snails, tadpoles and turtles that lived in and by the water below. Raccoons, muskrats, deer, fox, pheasants and other animals all came to drink there. One summer, because of drought the stream dried up to a mud slick. The garden blistered and withered and I remember how haggard, weathered and sweat-streaked my beloved dad was after a day on the tractor cultivating the meager corn crop in the dusty soil. Mom and the kids would take lunch out to him in the field, where beneath the shade of the tractor wheel he would gratefully drink Kool-aid from a jar.

Water to drink—even Kool-aid—was a precious thing and we all knew it. I remember how terrible it was when all the fish died in the creek or got stranded in small, smelly mud potholes. Though not much was said, Grandma and Grandpa carried such an air of anxiety, even a child could discern it. I watched Grandpa scan the odd, white rainless sky while Mom constantly kept vigil over us, not allowing us to play in the scorching sun. Every day we listened to the weather reports on the radio and heard how sometimes whole herds of cattle died from heat stroke. This was heartbreaking to me, and the reality of how sacred and precious water is became deeply ingrained in me.

Finally, as with all circular seasons in life, rains came and the drought ended. The creek flowed to brimming. I went wading in it, marveling at the new fish that found their way back from tributaries further upstream. The garden grew robust radishes, peas and carrots again and the meadow bloomed in the alfalfa field. *All this returning life was a result of the presence of water.* Our cistern filled, there was enough to drink for the horses and cows, and the land was no longer parched. I hold these memories to my heart and remember the lessons they bring. I remember what it was like not to have enough water and even today, when I empty a full bathtub of beautiful, soapy water down the drain, I feel a pang.

These life experiences as a child that taught me to revere water now help me to understand the dynamics of faith. I understand what a precious thing faith is and how vital it is to healing, hope and finding comfort and strength in life. Because of the tragedies I have known, I have come to see that faith as the living water of our souls can restore and renew us when grief and suffering have made us feel scorched and withered to the bone. Faith, like the tributaries upstream that rushed clear, life-giving water into our dried-up farm creek, consistently flows love and resilience into our empty inner reservoirs when we need it the most.

> *God who is a Bottomless Reservoir, remind us always that when we experience droughts of the soul, the Holy Spirit is like a well in a desert which will never run dry—waiting for us to drink deeply and flourish.*

He Said

On the first day of our church missionary trip to San Lucas Toliman in Guatemala, we were given an orientation to our new surroundings. We learned how precious the Mayans consider water and how scarce clean water is in this area of the world. This quaint, oppressed village is nestled adjacent to Lake Atitlan surrounded by mountains that reach the sky. The lake spreads its life-giving blanket in front of us. Here is where children swim and where mothers wash clothes. Without the lake, San Lucas might very well fade away.

Water is mentioned numerous times in the Bible. It is referred to metaphorically as a way to refresh and cleanse one's soul. Water is precious. It is a gift. Likewise, faith is a gift, something which is precious and nourishing. Like water, faith is needed to fully live. It provides us with the necessary nutrients for a true relationship with God.

—JPB

She Said

The strongest fear I ever felt literally caused my arms to burn during the day and my body to wake up in a cold, drenching sweat at night. These recurred because I didn't know how to get out of the "eye of the hurricane," how to battle the fear, and mostly the fear of the unknown. This earthly trial had revealed to me that I could no longer trust what I had seen and believed all my life. The only thing I could trust was something unseen and intangible. We turned to God.

My spouse and I prayed every morning and every night, first prayers by rote and then prayers from the heart. Eventually, God drew us so close that we could feel God's grace move through us when we requested peace from the Holy Spirit. Gradually, we worried less about what the newspapers and other media said and more about what God said, after all He knew us when we were knit in our mothers' wombs and He knew our heart . . . this is all that matters now or for eternity. Our mantra became, "God is good. He has given us so many blessings." Truly, although He could not take the persecution away from us, He had certainly made a way so that we could withstand any blows by praying God's word—which is the sword—and by relying on our internal reservoir of faith— which is our shield.

—SGB

Work Book Page

Discussion or Journal Questions

1. In our lives, we also experience times of famine and drought. When we feel as if we won't survive, it is good to remember that the love of God poured into our hearts is like the grain stored in the biblical story of Joseph. It is there to nourish, sustain, encourage and strengthen us.

    Talk about times of famine and times of great plenty you have experienced in your life. What do these times teach you about your dependence upon God and his ability to see you through?

2. Once, when I had to fast for a medical test, I could not have any water to drink until the test was over. I became excruciatingly thirsty, longing for even a chip of ice. *Physical, emotional* and *spiritual thirst* all stem from a longing for that which brings life and wholeness to body, mind and soul. Talk about these three kinds of thirst and experiences you have had with each type.

Goal

To explore what it means to rely on faith during times of personal drought and thirst.

Task

In John 7:37 Jesus says, "Let anyone who is thirsty come to me and let the one who believes in me drink." The next time you attend Mass, meditate upon the inner peace you have received as a result of going to communion and receiving both the bread and wine, the body and blood of Christ.

Prayer Image

Living water flowing from Christ's pierced side.

Affirmation Statement

When my inner reservoirs of strength and well-being are empty and dried up, faith flows the promise of better days to me from resurrections residing upstream.

—✳ The Colors of Life: ✳— Home at Last

Do not let your hearts be troubled . . .
In my Father's house there are many dwelling places.
If it were not so, would I have told you that I go to
prepare a place for you?   —John 14:1a,2

HAVING a degree in Interior Design has provided me with some interesting insights into the study of personal growth. It's interesting to review the changes in our preferences and how indicative these changes can be of inner transitions. In the early 1970s, I couldn't get enough color; everything was purple and red with dramatic red carpeting and Gothic wallpaper with lots of white wicker accessories and black, wrought iron railings throughout the house. I was in my early twenties and happily married with one son. I enjoyed making impressions and I liked being different from everyone else—which is a hallmark of young adults as they discover themselves and assert their individuality.

By the time I was in my middle to late twenties, I had already phased out the red carpet and replaced it with champagne. I softened my passion for purple to lavender as I processed the death of my beloved dad, and not long after our middle son was born, I instinctively began to understand the importance of the sacred space I created in my home. My faith deepened and I experienced a spiritual awakening following my grief and new motherhood. Life seemed to take on a new color and was saturated with meaning, depth and richness. I was always lighting candles, playing soft music and our third son was born, completing our beautiful family.

In my thirties, another life-changing challenge came upon us. My mom, like my dad, had developed colon cancer and after a year-long battle died, leaving me heartbroken. Everything in my décor during the following year became beige. Life temporarily lost its luster and my external decorating was reflective of my internal sorrow. A few years later, when I found myself facing a midlife crisis, we redid the whole house in mauve. I became a full-fledged antique lover and felt drawn to pieces that had character and history and which had "seen" life. As new horizons stretched me, the color I fell in love with was hunter green, the symbol of new life and hope. I began to understand the seasons of life and how the joys, adversity and sorrows we experience widen our scope, faith and creativity for living. I was coming into my own as a woman and my home reflected this new-found maturity and harmony.

Then, more challenges followed when I lost my health. Life got cloudy for a time until I learned to redefine myself again. Out went the mauve and along with a handicap ramp and safety railings, in came black, Victorian floral carpet and lovely leather furniture. The wallpaper reflected a tropical theme expressing the inner freedom I gradually experienced as I mastered the art of coping with disabilities. The process took years, and I thought at last that no more bad things could happen; contentment settled in as I watched my beloved family growing up and I learned to spiritually surrender heartaches and limitations that I couldn't change.

Then, the unthinkable happened. Our third son, Mic, died and the world fell apart. It took years for my family to begin to feel whole again. As gentle but persistent healing gradually embraced us, my decorating reflected our altered lives. Again, I was drawn to a new color I had never used before—this time a deep, beautiful shade called February Gold which reflected the amber in our stained glass windows. Seeing the golden glow of this color each morning made me feel that the sun was rising in our souls again; and that we were being embraced and comforted.

As I reflected on all the changes our home had seen, I realized the evolving nature of life and that nothing stays the same—as after thirty-one years of marriage, through the temporary shambles my marital separation ushered in, I left my home and began creating a new sacred space in an apartment. For my children, I realized more than ever, that home was more than a building—but where the hearts of our family dwell. That was the one thing that did not change—and the most beautiful to me.

> *Divine Creator of Many Mansions, the joy we take in creating our earthly homes is a reflection of the joy you feel as you prepare for our final homecoming. . . where at last, we will all dwell with you and you with us. . . home at last.*

He Said

Planning for the arrival of our son Josiah was exciting, although it meant giving up my office space for his bedroom. My wife was adamant that we needed lots of color in the room because it stimulated newborns and encouraged creativity. One by one she coaxed each of our new son's 27 cousins into his room. Their task was to write their name somewhere on the wall and put their handprints or a design nearby using a palette of bright colors. The artistic flairs soared: Victoria alternated colors with the letters of her name; Mike, Jr. 16, painted his childhood name "Mikey," and Shelley his oldest cousin from California used pink lettering under a bright orange sun. The little kids squealed while dipping their hands in the paint and stamping them on the wall. This multi-colored rainbow room never failed to jolt us awake each morning!

Watching children choose and use paints brought me heart-warming joy. Being able to recognize the wide diversity of colors that surround our life is also a blessing. Just like people, colors are not the same and have different appeal. Who knows why one person chooses the staid navy blue car while another gravitates toward sporty red? Noting that our color preferences change over the years, I am reminded how much it is like our spiritual journey whose hues deepen and fade depending on where we are on our walk with God.

—JPB

She Said

I was nervous and a bit scared as I joined the long procession line slowly inching up to the casket. Our beloved Father Greg had succumbed to death eighty days after his double lung and kidney transplant. I didn't want to be here, but I wanted the experience of "saying goodbye before we said hello again." Reaching the altar, there he lay . . . in a simple line-grooved pine box . . . dressed regally in the attire he frequently wore. . . a plain white garment. The only splash of color was a brilliant Guatemalan scarf around his neck which graced the length of his gown.

In the pew, I read in the memorial booklet about his deep admiration for the Trappist movement and how he had tried to emulate their simple lifestyle. During the service, I heard wondering whispers on why Father Greg had shiny black shoes on instead of the sandals he usually sported. The next Sunday, this question was fielded from the pulpit. "And for those of you who thought that it odd or strange that Father Greg had those black, shiny shoes on with the rest of his humble garb, I assure you there was no mistake. This was Father Greg's request and he wanted to make sure we'd follow it. . . he insisted on having them on when he went to Heaven. They were his dancing shoes."   —*SGB*

Work Book Page

Discussion or Journal Questions

1. In *The Rock That is Higher,* Madeleine L' Engle writes, "We are all strangers in a strange land, longing for home, but not quite knowing what or where home is. We glimpse it sometimes in our dreams, or as we turn a corner, and suddenly there is a strange, sweet familiarity that vanishes almost as soon as it comes."

   Talk about the home you now live in, former homes and what makes a house or building feel like a home to you.

2. What is your first memory of color? Talk about emotions certain colors evoke in you or messages certain colors seem to carry.

Goal

To explore the many dimensions of what it means to have a home and to be a home.

Task

In his award-winning book, *Spirituality @ Work: 10 Ways to Balance your Life on the Job,* Greg Pierce offers thoughts on the discipline of surrounding ourselves with sacred objects: "A sacred object can be anything from a piece of traditional religious art to a photo of family and friends, or it can be a completely secular item that carries for us a very deep and spiritual meaning."

   Talk about the sacred spaces in your life, objects that have special meaning and ways that you could better attune yourself to your surroundings. How does clutter affect your spaces? What does the phrase "to be at home wherever you are" mean to you?

Prayer Image

Change of Address mailing labels from the post office.

Affirmation Statement

I will not fool myself into thinking any earthly sacred space or dwelling is permanent—but are rather just shadows and shadings of my future heavenly home.

~ 19 ~

—✻ Woman on Walkabout: ✻— A Time to Halt

Walk about Zion, go all around it. . . that you may tell the next generation that this is God, our God . . . our guide forever. —Psalm 48:12, 13b, 14

IN the outback regions of Australia, aborigines go on Walkabout quests to seek a spiritual experience, make a rite of passage or to commune with solitude. As Ernestine Hill once described it in 1943, "At last, the loneliness that they have valued far above takes them to itself. . . " A number of years ago, I, too made an inner Walkabout as I resided in a hospital following surgery, lost in a blur of events which I was powerless to control. Early on I wrote, "I am in the outback, barefoot, on a solo Walkabout, picking up rocks as I go . . . searching—searching for strength. The inner weather of this illness is buffeting, unrelenting, like a dry, searing wind. I scan the horizons of my soul with hands cupped across my eyes, wondering what direction I should go. I have 'gone bush' to find out, envisioning sand between my toes while nurses, IV's and needles fill my days but not the journey."

I found it helpful to frame the medical crisis I was experiencing into a spiritual quest and the Walkabout concept proved to be a cre-ative coping technique that kept my mind active within the barren days of tests and pain. *"Keep Walking. . . "* I kept telling myself, imag-ining passing through Ezekiel's Valley of Dry Bones as the crisis continued. I had given up on prayers for strength, which seemed unanswered, and switched to prayers for endurance. Marlo Morgan wrote of her own Walkabout in *Mutant Messages Down Under*, "The sky above was a cobalt canopy speckled with silver. I thought about my adventure. A door had opened and I had entered a world I didn't know existed." The only difference was, my canopy was acoustical tile. I remained determined to transcend, to walk the walk wherever that took me.

I was traveling through the swirling, misty places that only the very ill can know. When I heard a small voice of panic taunting, "You aren't going to get better," I would chant hopefully to myself, "I am strong, I am healing," even when I didn't feel it. Finally, the day came when my Walkabout felt too wearying for me to continue. I was at a crossroads—exhausted—my inner resources used up. Morgan had written, "The bush flies in the outback are horrendous. The hordes appear with the first rays of sunlight. They infest the sky, traveling in black packs of what seems to be millions. I could not help eating and breathing flies." Her guide Oota said to her, "Humans cannot exist if everything that is unpleasant is eliminated instead of understood. When the flies come, we surrender."

Surrender. The word felt like a cooling breeze or a soothing balm. In the margins of my notebook, I drew a small tent. "Make camp," I wrote. "At last. What a difference a day makes, or a week, or a series of weeks. That is something to hold on to. *Believe.* Nothing stays exactly the same indefinitely. Change can come in the form of silent nuance. I needed that miracle. While I do not yet feel the healing, perhaps this is its forerunner: an overshadowing wing that has come to wait with me."

It was an unbelievable relief to halt. As I sketched a sign that said *"Stop Now, "* I felt I had permission to just be. There is a great vastness in the human spirit, its land stretches forever. I never came close to finding a final horizon; however I felt that I had communed with the eternal comfort within. This was what I had been searching for all along, and as I closed the circle on the amazing, horrendous Walkabout experience from my hospital bed, I wrote, "Be faithful to the process. Enduring can be learned. There is an ageless voice of strength from within. Believe in the Silent Nuance. There is a time to halt, to be taken care of and to do nothing but dwell in the fullness and safety of spiritual surrender." As Marlo Morgan wrote:

> Born empty handed
> Die empty handed
> I witnessed life at its fullest
> Empty handed.

At the bottom of the page, I appreciatively drew a final sign that said, *"Don't Give Up. The wise never walk alone, they walk with God."* All these years later, the message remains as powerful as the day I received it.

> *God Who Breathes Life into Old, Dry Bones, even more*
> *so, through calling us to rest, do you delight in breathing*
> *the fullness of life and breath into old, dry faith.*

He Said

I've always been envious of college professors who take a sabbatical – a break from their life routine to pursue reflection and fulfillment of particular professional goals. Although our society promotes vacation as time to ourselves, often times they are too short and include an itinerary so packed that you need a vacation to recover from the vacation. I am talking about an extended period of time when we can truly remove ourselves from our current world to gain perspective. Sometimes life presents us with opportunities, but we fail to realize it. A job layoff, time in a hospital, or time in a prison are opportunities for self-reflection. Although they appear negative in root, they can be very positive in terms of growth.

We can also build mini-sabbaticals into our lives. These "quiet times" are scheduled times to exclusively meet with our Lord and pray and reflect. Does your church have a chapel, or a designated prayer time? Do you have a quiet space or chair where you can sit and meditate, converse with God? What better way to shut out the chaos of daily life than to create sacred prayer time? The best thing is that you don't have to say a word, just relax and enjoy the peaceful feeling that will come as you trust in the love the Lord has for you and ask Him to carry your burdens. —*JPB*

She Said

When I'm running away from something, like stress, I go jogging. When I'm running toward something, like an answer, I go walking. And when I walk I often go to the big cottonwood tree I've adopted as a listening tree. I walk and walk and by the time I reach the cottonwood tree, I sit and listen for the answer to my question. Sometimes it comes immediately, sometimes it comes later in my walk or even later in the week. But the answer does come. Faith assures it.

A wise old friend of mine recently reminded me, "If you want to meet God, you have to get in the dirt." She was referring to gardening but I truly understood this analogy. God created earth and the closer we can get to each of His creations, the closer we feel to Him. A whispering cottonwood tree reminds me of God's voice, the whisper of angels, the eternity of time. There is wisdom in nature.

—*SGB*

Work Book Page

Discussion or Journal Questions

1. Talk about a time when you had to surrender to circumstances beyond your control and stop searching. How can you tell when God is calling you to stillness? Which is harder, recognizing the need or doing it? Has it ever occurred to you that a choice is being offered you that requires a response?

2. In his excellent book, *Sabbath Moments: Finding Rest for the Soul in the Midst of Daily Living*, Adolfo Quezada writes, "We need to monitor ourselves because we are the only ones who know when it is time to stop. When we listen to the cues and dare to stop for a while, we discover that it not just physical restoration that we need, but also spiritual reconnection. It is when we have become still and quiet that we hear God speak to us." Talk about a time when you experienced a special sense of kinship with God in stillness.

Goal

To evaluate your energy levels and if needed, devise a responsible plan that includes proper physical, mental and spiritual rest.

Task

Adolfo teaches that "We do not have to wait until we are utterly drained and exhausted before we rest. We can prevent fatigue by resting, rather than resting to alleviate fatigue. We rest because it is our nature to stop our activity and restore our energies." Talk about your present lifestyle, the amount of rest you get and specific changes you could make to improve and renew your energy levels.

Prayer Image

A still lake.

Affirmation Statement

I will not feel guilty when I need to stop activity to renew my energies, but will look upon it as a divine rhythm God calls me to.

~ 20 ~

A Tribute to a Mother-in-law: Celebrating a Legacy of Faith

But Naomi said to her two daughters-in-law,
". . . May the Lord deal kindly with you,
as you have dealt with . . . me."
. . . Then she kissed them . . . —Ruth 1:8,9

WHEN I became a mother-in-law, I began trying to educate myself in the happy, complex dynamics of this new life phase. Looking back, I remember when I was a young bride in 1972 and getting to know my own mother-in-law. I realize how life comes full circle and I think about what it is like for my mother-in-law now, experiencing yet another rite of passage, as a resident in a nursing home. Through example, she has paved a wise and caring path that offers insight into how to be a mother-in-law. My earliest memory is when she had me model my wedding dress for her own mother at the nursing home where she resided. I remember twirling in my gown and noting the unconscious devotion my mother-in-law had for her mother and for her mother-in-law who lived nearby.

Through the years, I observed how my mother-in-law treated all her in-laws as if they were her own children—respectful, friendly and with good manners. Birthdays for everyone were celebrated the same, with a homemade cake and presents including the ritual gifts of underwear, socks and dish towels. Here, I learned the importance of tradition that my mother-in-law so beautifully created and carried on. For wedding anniversaries, without fail she sent a card and gift of money. Christmas was always painstakingly prepared for, with the proverbial oyster stew. For the in-laws who hadn't learned to like it, she always included something else. This brought in a third lesson: her flexibility and genuine efforts to please those she cared about.

She rarely, if ever, spoke a bad word about anyone, worked hard all her life, never complained and always took life in stride, even through the challenging times. Her way of approaching life carried the message, "don't give up." Even when her husband died and she got breast cancer, she picked up the pieces and pressed forward with courage, inspiring those around her. She never had an enemy in the world and lived life with a genuine zest and resilience of spirit.

My mother-in-law adored parades, ice cream cones, fireworks, visitors and traveling. One of her greatest joys was to go to the lake each summer to stay in rented cabins with her family. I remember her literally drinking in every shining moment with joyful abandonment to the happiness she felt. This brought yet another lesson: to revel in the moment and savor life, which she certainly did. She was a "saver" and I remember opening the refrigerator one time and finding a bowl with three peas in it! She saved wrapping paper, ribbon, cards and was extremely frugal and mindful of the value of things. Always a caretaker by nature, she seemed to know what is important in life and could be counted on to bring brownies to a sick neighbor, gifts to a baby shower or help at a funeral luncheon.

The phrase "God's Love is Like a Grandma" fits my mother-in-law perfectly. She was a devoted grandmother who delighted in her grandchildren. I have many memories of her hanging fragrant sheets on the clothesline on a cool summer's morning—with visiting grandchildren nearby, swinging on the swing set or playing with the farm kittens that she always fed. I remember her in pedal pushers and her comfy work shoes, riding her bike up to get the mail, or canning, cooking and baking, with rollers in her hair as she listened to music on the radio. She loved to sit on the screened-in porch on warm summer evenings, soaking her feet after a long day, resting and gazing out on the farm yard with the expanse of stars behind the barn. This taught another lesson: it is good to just be and reflect after the satisfaction of a good work day.

My mother-in-law adored her friends. She loved playing cards, going to birthday club and teaching CCD. She always looked for the good in people, was forgiving, fun-loving, earnest and spontaneous. She loved dancing, never put on airs and always tried to be a peacemaker if someone in the family wasn't getting along. She believed in second chances and giving people the benefit of the doubt. Perhaps as a mother-in-law, the greatest lesson she has taught me is to live life to its fullest. My greatest hope is to carry on her legacy to my own daughter-in-laws as a gift of appreciation to the woman my mother-in-law always was and spiritually still is, as she lives with her life's last challenge: Alzheimer's disease.

God Who is the Epitome of Nurturance, bless and keep mothers-in-law, fathers-in-law, daughters-in-law and sons-in-law everywhere with a special understanding of generosity and good will that always transcends differences.

He Said

I have always despised mother-in-law stereotypes—the ones painting mother-in-laws as busy bodies and old battle-axes. I detested these because I witnessed how my own mother warmly embraced my older sisters' new husbands and accepted them. She honored the choice of her daughters and she also made sure our expanded family got along and grew together.

When I married, I saw the institution of mother-in-law twofold. I marveled at how my mom accepted my wife as her own daughter and I realized the true blessing of being accepted into a new family by a wonderful mother-in-law. Family events grew to be very special—more people at the holiday dinner table, more laughter and stories, cooing sounds of newborns, and love overflowing. Both mom and mother-in-law glowed whenever their families gathered, temporarily forgetting their pain of being widows and alone. Yet, at peace, because God had never left them.　　—*JPB*

She Said

It was a snowy, icy day, and I ran back into my in-laws home to get my husband. My car was stuck on a patch of ice. Joe came out and right next to him, was his mother Sophie. "We'll get you out of here in no time!" she confidently proclaimed. Gloveless she pushed on the cold metal of the car along with my husband. Back and forth they rocked me until *floosh* my car flew off the patch of ice and onto drier asphalt.

This particular instance reminds me of the vigor and vitality of my mother-in-law. Sophie was "hip," tasting and savoring every ounce of life like a perfect filet mignon. She fussed with her appearance, insisted on knowing the latest fashions, tried out new recipes weekly; she golfed and cross-country skied in her 70s and never once declined an offer to go for a ride, a trip or an adventure. Although she faced many tragedies, including losing three family members in one year, she never lost her zest for life. Now at 82, she is in a nursing home with stroke-induced dementia, and even there, her friendly demeanor and lively personality still shines. No doubt God is still working through her to minister to us and those around her.   —*SGB*

Work Book Page

1. Shortly before Christmas 2003—the fifth one without our son—I had an incredible dream, the most amazing one I've ever had. I dreamt I was walking down a road in the summertime. Suddenly, I came upon a long, white fence. On the other side of the fence was a lake and trees; wading at the shore up to his knees with a fishing rod and reel in hand was Mic. I immediately started crying, saying, "I miss you so deeply." He only smiled in a lovely way and said like it was no big deal, "Oh, I'm around," and with a big grin, *"I am as happy as a person can get."* Mic, like my mother-in-law was always a happy person in life and while it is not the natural order of things, he will be among those meeting her when it is her time to cross the white fence. Even though she is basically unresponsive now and rarely speaks, she will not be this way on the other side. Rather, she will be her fullest, highest self—and it is very easy to imagine her laughing as she always did.

   Talk about dreams, coincidences or happenings that have suggested to you that loved ones who have died are visiting and encouraging you.

2. Kneel by your bedside before you go to bed tonight and offer a litany of *God Bless* prayers, saying each person's name who comes to mind as a way of loving, blessing, releasing, forgiving and thanking each one for what they brought to your life.

Goal

To learn to receive, extend and reciprocate a legacy of goodwill and faith to those who go before us and who follow in our footsteps.

Task

One of my favorite quotes in Ann Dawson's *A Season of Grief,* is from Archbishop Fisher (former Archbishop of Canterbury), "I never think of a friend after his death as now resting in a sleep of peace. I cannot believe that he has passed to the state of personal inactivity which the words suggest. I am more completely sure that he has passed to more life and more activity, to a state of greatly increased spiritual awareness and exercise."

What messages would you like to leave behind when it's your turn to cross that fence? Write it down and put it in a safe place so it can be included at your funeral celebration.

Image

A torch bearer.

Affirmation Statement

I will live my journey of faith as a conscious legacy of love and healing poured out for those who will follow in my footsteps needing light for the path.

Part Three

Living the Truth

Those who walk blamelessly and do what is right, and speak the truth from their heart . . . shall never be moved.

—Psalm 15:2, 5b

Spiritual empowerment is evident in our lives by our willingness to tell ourselves the truth, to listen to the truth when it's told to us and to dispense the truth as lovingly as possible, when we feel compelled to talk from the heart.   —*Christine Baldwin*

There are few human beings who receive the truth, complete and staggering, by instant illumination. Most of them acquire it fragment by fragment, on a small scale by successive developments, cellularly, like a laborious mosaic.   —*Anais Nin*

There is no joy
like the joy of being a voice
for the voiceless.
There is no peace
like the peace that comes
from speaking the truth.

—*Macrina Wiederkehr*
Seasons of Your Heart

~ 21 ~

⟶❈ Beyond Hatred: ❈⟵ Spiritual Victors

Beloved, let us love one another because love is from God; . . . God is love, and those who abide in love abide in God, and God abides in them. —1 John 4:7A, 16B

"**H**ATRED is a multi-layered emotion with vast implications," a friend once said. "We are taught that hate is bad, wrong and evil. But when we feel it, there is no mistaking it. It's simply there and we have to decide what to do with it." Once when I harbored bad thoughts toward a false friend who had betrayed me deeply and said crushing, cruel lies about me that cut to the core, I envisioned an image of huge black-clawed talons with me in its clutches.

My life was significantly altered and changed by the self-serving actions of this troubled woman and initially, I felt devastated, shocked and numb with disbelief. "This can't have happened," I kept thinking. No wonder I had envisioned the talons, I was caught in the clutches of someone else's struggle with pain, neediness and dissatisfaction in life—that really had little to do with me. The truth was, I was just not that significant in her eyes. . . my feelings did not matter to my so-called friend. The appalling deception and unfairness of what had happened to me ushered in feelings I had never encountered before. I was outraged.

Knowing I needed to find the wisdom, strength and power to deal with how I was feeling, I decided to do what is called an

Inquiry. I wrote in my notebook, "What is the spirituality of hate?" Then, I went to a thesaurus and wrote down words that described hate, such as: to detest, loathe, scorn, feel repulsion for, bear a grudge against, denounce and hold in contempt. It was sobering to realize that these feelings and all their cousins would gladly make a home in me if I allowed that to happen.

As I began studying how to become spiritually victorious over betrayal, I found myself on a quest that ultimately changed my life. Reading books and poetry by many great authors began to expand my perspective as I discovered how truly heroic men and women can be in transcending, positively channeling and redeeming feelings of hatred. By setting boundaries and becoming pro-active, I found I could actually monitor resentment—not allowing it to invade the ground I gained. 2 Corinthians 10:5 talks about the importance of taking our thoughts captive by consciously restricting non-life-giving reflection. I simultaneously learned the value of this as I invested in a spiritual recovery that did not encourage the suppression of feelings—but rather the release of them.

Further perspective was gained when I read the words of Morrie Schwartz in *Tuesdays with Morrie,* "But detachment doesn't mean you don't let the experience penetrate you. On the contrary, you let it penetrate you *fully.* That's how you are able to leave it." He goes on to explain that when we hold back emotions and don't allow ourselves to go all the way through them—we never get detached, because we're too busy being afraid of the vulnerability that loving can entail. Even though it was challenging for me to trust again and it took some time, I instinctively knew that God was calling me to resilience, receptivity to life and others—and mature, spiritual empowerment that can take heartache and betrayal in stride.

The bad experience that brought about my resentment remained a bad experience. It should not have happened and was morally wrong. However, by doing the prayer work and not wasting the lessons, I found that grace offered me an opportunity to decide who I wanted to be, independent of the actions of others. As Sue Monk Kidd wrote in *The Secret Life of Bees,* "When you're unsure of yourself . . . when you start pulling back into doubt and small living, . . . Get up from there and live like the glorious girl you are." Referring to the Black Madonna in the story, Kidd writes, "She's the power inside you, understand? And whatever it is that keeps widening your heart. . . when you get down to it, Lily, that's the only purpose grand enough for a human life. Not just to love—but to *persist* in love."

In the book of Daniel, chapter 12, we read of many who are purified, cleansed and refined. Verse 11 reads, "Happy are those who persevere . . . go your way and rest; you shall rise for your reward at the end of days." It is the word *persevere* that links not only the biblical passage but the journey of our hearts. God bless our coming and going, our pain and our recovery; may we persist in allowing and trusting the love and generosity of God to transform not only ourselves—but those who have lost the way.

Resilient, Empowering God of Our Highest Good, thank you for reminding us that to live in love and truth is not to place ourselves 'above' anyone but to change the energy, which has its source in You.

He Said

After serving as a full-time city council member of a large city for ten years, one facet I never understood was that some people intensely disliked me without ever knowing me or my views. For one reason or another the fact that I was a "politician" was cause enough to hate me. The longer I was in office, the thicker my skin became. Like many of my colleagues, I received hate mail, threats, and was prey to malicious rumors. By focusing on what I could accomplish, it was easier to persevere despite the vibes of hate I often felt.

I remember one decision in particular where a landowner and I locked horns. It concerned whether or not to support construction of a warehouse on a vacant river property. I preferred housing or open space, but the property was in private hands and zoned for industrial use. On a cold and rainy Saturday night a few weeks before the council vote, I walked the site comparing my vision with the landowner's. A voice asked, "What is really best for this area?" Startled, I turned to see the landowner next to me. For a change, it was just the two of us . . . no partisan crowds . . . no bureaucratic staff. We went to a nearby coffee shop and as we talked, I learned he was a kind and gentle man; he realized I cared about my community and its future and that my decision was not personal. Slowly that palpable barrier of hate began to fall away like the blue ice from an iceberg as we warmed to each other's viewpoints. Slowly our conversation turned to "our" city's severe housing shortage and before long, he began to formulate plans on building moderately priced housing instead of an industrial warehouse.

—JPB

She Said

Busily, I was doing the monthly bills and very proud of myself that I was ahead of time. "Whew," I said as I filed the last statement in my file drawer, "I'm sure glad that's done." Then as I went to gather the bills that I had signed, stamped and sealed, they were nowhere to be found. I looked everywhere . . . on top my desk, in my desk, in every file they could be and all others, too. I seethed with anger . . . at myself for being so careless. The next day I even looked through the garbage and the recycling! The anger allowed me no perspective, just self-loathing. After three days, one of the bills was due, so I finally gave in and wrote another check for that one. Each day, I hunted in a new place and retraced the old places. *Finally*, I gave up, "That's it! Wherever they are, I'm done looking!" As soon as I surrendered, anger flowed from me like water from an unleashed dam. Chastisement and browbeating washed away. I had forgiven myself and a calming peace returned.

Of course, you know what happened next. Within the hour, I went to move an emergency kit from the stairway and underneath lay the missing bills. Picking them up, I nonchalantly put them in the post. Real power was in the surrender not in the struggle, just as Christ had demonstrated on the cross. Once I surrendered, I could let go of self-hatred and move forward.   —*SGB*

Work Book Page

Discussion or Journal Page

1. Once I was so mad at my younger sister I shouted, "I hate you!" My mother remarked quietly, "You should never say those words—if your sister suddenly died, 'I hate you' would be your last words to her, and you would always feel bad about it." Even at the age of six, I remember feeling chilled at such a thought and I never forgot my mother's wise words. Can you recall the first time you said or felt you hated someone? How did it make you feel?

2. In one of His most beautiful and far-reaching sermons, Jesus ushered in a New Age when He said, "Blessed are those who are persecuted for righteousness' sake, for theirs is the kingdom of heaven. Blessed are you when people revile you and persecute you and utter all kinds of evil against you falsely on my account. Rejoice and be glad, for your reward is great in heaven . . ." (Mt 5:10-12).

   Read the Beatitudes often and talk about ways these words encourage you.

Goal

To examine ways to be a spiritual victor when hateful feelings and experiences arise.

Task

When we are in the midst of a trial, remembering those who have gone before us and not only survived but thrived gives us courage. Make a list of those who have known hate, prejudice, injustice—seeming failure for any number of reasons—but through perseverance have found a peaceful and happy life. Let the examples help you to take heart. What role do you think grace plays in those who find restoration?

Prayer Image

The restoration of Job at the end of his life.

Affirmation Statement

Rather than reciprocating meanness and hatred with meanness and hatred, I will be victorious in all situations by refusing to allow bitterness to be my message to the world.

22

⟶ Incubation: ⟵
Times of Waiting

. . . your God will make you abundantly prosperous in
all your undertakings,
in the fruit of your body, in the fruit of your livestock
and in the fruit of your soil.
For the Lord will again take delight in prospering you,
just as he delighted in prospering your ancestors.

—Deuteronomy 30:9

TIMES of waiting teach us the dynamics of patience which are mysteriously necessary to all that is becoming. Gertrude Mueller Nelson writes, ". . . nothing of value comes into being without a period of quiet incubation: not a healthy baby, not a loving relationship, not a reconciliation, a new understanding, a work of art, never a transformation. Rather, a shortened period of incubation brings forth what is not whole or even alive. Brewing, baking, simmering, fermenting, ripening, germinating, gestating are the feminine processes of becoming and they are symbolic states of being which belong in a life of value, necessary for transformation."

The discipline of patience and delayed gratification is never easy for me, especially when I am working on a book. As I begin each one, I place an egg in a brass cup by my computer and leave it there for about a year or more as a symbol of the spiritual incubation and work I am doing. Then, when I feel the time is right, after the book is published, I release the egg in a stream and ask God to bless the work, keep it safe, take care of it and bring it to fruition where it needs to be. I release trying to control its destiny and ask for the trust that it takes to spiritually relinquish it.

After my book, *Meditations for Survivors of Suicide* came out, I walked down to a creek with my egg in tow. It was dusk and even though the stream was basically frozen, water about six inches deep was rushing through giant culverts, so tall you could walk in them. I prayerfully stood there, reluctant to throw in my egg because I felt such maternal, protective attachment to it. Finally, I gently touched it to my lips and dropped it in. When it hit the water, it broke. I watched as the egg went tumbling away, while the broken piece remained behind, sinking to the shallow bottom. Suddenly, as I watched, a whirl of current caught it and away it went, out of my sight. I immediately understood the spiritual lesson of letting go of our brokenness, and realizing that both our joys and sorrows get caught up in the stream of life that carries us, along with our hopes, dreams and losses to the heart of God.

Releasing an egg is also, in many ways, like a rite of passage; as I crawled up the steep, dried grassy embankment and crossed the road to view the water rushing through the other side of the culvert, it was like crossing a road in my heart to a new place. When I got home, I excitedly and with a very sacred feeling, got a new egg out of the refrigerator and put it in the brass cup—a symbol of Something New—and the hopeful incubating I was doing as the book you now hold unfolded and I envisioned the fruits of my hard labors. The process was like a miracle to me and always has been. The miracle of birth comes to us in many, many ways.

Sue Monk Kidd writes of incubation and birth, "Whenever new life grows and emerges, darkness is crucial to the process. Whether it's the caterpillar in the chrysalis, the seed in the ground, the child in the womb or the True Self in the soul, there's always a time of waiting in the dark. . . . with every birth there is a womb, and if we want to find the inner kingdom, we will have to enter the place of waiting, darkness and incubation." It is our glorious inner kingdom from which gestation stems—our holy of holies—the place from which our dreams, children, books and all things beautiful emerge. Grant us the patience, God, to wait; bless and honor the gifts that only we can bring to the world through the spark of your divine inspiration that takes root in the soil of our hearts.

> *God Who Rested on the Seventh Day, you remind us by your own example: life is a beautiful cycle of rest, womb and incubation time . . . fruition . . . rest, womb, incubation . . .*

He Said

As fathers of growing children the same age, a group of us doting Dads enjoyed getting together. It was fun for us and the children and it also gave the Moms a well-deserved break. In the cool of these spring evenings it was a joyous sight watching our children riding their bicycles with training wheels across the park, their fluorescent helmets wobbling like jello. And, just as young birds leave their nest to learn to fly, soon a few of the children wanted to ride without training wheels. Their success inspired others and soon all but one was riding independently. The lone holdout was my son, Josiah. While the other five-year-olds zoomed by, Josiah quipped, "Dad, my time will come" and refused any offer of help. Amazingly, he seemed to keep up with the other kids and as his feet pedaled feverishly, I could almost hear the "da-da-da-da-da-da" music of the wicked witch riding her bike in the Wizard of Oz.

The summer of Josiah's sixth birthday, the same group of families took a trip together for a week. Hoping to encourage him to ride without training wheels, we took them off and lowered the seat to make sure his feet could touch the ground. Every day he sat on his bike and watched the other kids. Still, he refused help reassuring me, "My time will come, Dad." The day before we were to go home, he sat on his bike and coasted down the asphalt path in front of the cabin. Next he coasted and pedaled a bit, crashed and cried. But he got up again and again and again. Finally, he accepted help with me at the top of the "hill" (small incline) and his mom at the bottom of the hill. In an hour he was riding circles around the place as if he'd done it all his life. Truly, "his time had come."

—JPB

She Said

Nervously I waited for the teacher to come into our classroom . . . at 17 I had left my family and small town of 90 people, moved to the Twin Cities of 300,000, and was now on the first day at Vo-Tech to become a legal secretary. When I looked around to see who was kicking my chair, I came face to face with a beautiful brown-eyed girl with dark braids. "Hi. My name is Linda," she shyly whispered. "Hi, Linda, my name is Sheila." And that's all we had time for before our instructor walked in. Slowly, we developed a familiarity, an acquaintance, then a friendship. Linda, who was from Minneapolis, welcomed me to her group of friends and four of us gals started hanging out together. Over the next seven years our relationships grew as we shared our lives, our loves and our hopes for the future.

Little could I fathom how that first "hi" from Linda would affect my life. She was the one to introduce me to my future husband, Joe. She was also the one who confided that Joe had romantic feelings for me. Marrying a year apart, Linda and I were bridesmaids in each other's weddings. Flash forward 17 years and I am with my husband at a law firm after he has just been indicted and is scheduled for a press conference. I have not dressed for the occasion and need to find a blazer to put over my shirt. Suddenly, the image of Linda comes to mind and I realize she is here in this very building where she has worked for years as a legal secretary. I gratefully borrow her blazer for the TV cameras. Months later I am sitting in a small room at the courthouse as a sequestered witness. Feeling alone, I respond to the knock at the door and once again I am face to face with Linda. She has a big pot of hot water in one hand and assorted teas in the other, which she has carried *10 blocks* from her office. What a relief to see a friendly, familiar face! As always, she is quiet and listens to my ramblings. So glad am I, Lord, for the sojourners in my life such as Linda. Ah incubation . . . the process of getting to know the other person's heart and caring about what happens to them. . . it is a glorious journey and the reward is rock solid friendship.   —*SGB*

Work Book Page

Discussion or Journal Questions

1. The journey of writing this book is a story in itself. I never dreamed the incubation of it would involve a turbulent, life-altering rite of passage in my life regarding my marriage. Like the egg that broke in the culvert that day, so did the work on this book experience a place of complete and utter brokenness. Whole pieces of it sunk to the bottom of my heart and beautiful material no longer usable went tumbling away in a current I had no control over. Surrendering to the brokenness this book experienced was a horrendous grief process for me as I erased whole sections of it from my computer. When I moved, I took my computer with me, put a new egg in the brass cup and began the waiting all over again. At the end of the year, I wrote that the miracle I gestated was the birth of my own transformed life. I not only survived but so did this beloved book—both of us deeper and wiser than before.

    Talk about new life, accomplishments or transformations you have experienced following extended periods of waiting or brokenness.

2. The Parable of the Sower is one of the most beloved in the Bible. The books of Matthew, Mark and Luke all relate the story of a sower who went to sow his seed, which represented the word of God. Some fell on the path and was trampled, some was eaten by birds, some fell on rocks or among thorns and some fell on good soil, where it grew and produced a hundred fold. "But as for that in the good soil, these are the ones who, when they hear the word, hold it fast in an honest and good heart, and bear fruit with patient endurance" Luke 8:15.

    Talk about the word of God in your life. Do you read the Bible? Do the stories and people come alive for you in a real

143

way that offers assistance and companionship? If you were to portray yourself as a sower of seeds during times of waiting, how would you describe the soil in which you sow? What spiritual value do you see in darkness?

Goal

To learn to spiritualize times of waiting, allowing it to incubate wisdom, transformation and/or new beginnings and to visualize the spiritual wealth that can arise from the tiniest of seeds of faith sown.

Task

Many years ago, I had a necklace that held a tiny mustard seed encased in a piece of resin attached to the chain. As I incubate precious memories, I wish I still had it. Memorize the following Bible verse from Luke 13:18-19: "What is the Kingdom of God like? And to what should I compare it? It is like a mustard seed that someone took and sowed in the garden; it grew and became a tree, and the birds of the air made nests in its branches." Discuss this beautiful imagery. In what ways does it encourage you?

Prayer Image

A tulip bulb beneath the snow.

Affirmation Statement

When I must wait uncertainly in the dark for guidance, revelations and for life to unfold, I will be as a germinating seed, filled with potential for great love and a magnificent life that blesses.

23

⟶⟶ Walking on Water: ⟵⟵
Taking Risks

Do not fear. . . when you pass through the waters, I will
be with you;   —Isaiah 43:1b, 2

A NUMBER of years ago, I experienced one of my greatest
lessons in risk-taking when a friend and I attended an aquatic class for handicapped people. We had some initial trepidation, but by the time we'd gotten into our swimsuits in the locker room, met the nurturing, supportive teachers and slid into the water, we were grinning. The water temperature was ideal, slipping like liquid silk across my skin. We relaxed as the water lapped gently to our chins while buoying us as our instructor took us through the warm-up walk. It felt exhilarating to be in the shimmering pool, and as we all held hands and helped each other along, I felt like I never wanted to get out. Within ten minutes, however, my muscles began weakening, and I found myself unable to walk or get out of the pool without assistance. It was shocking! I sat on the edge of the pool biting my lip and trying not to cry. I went back to the classes several more times, but the same thing always happened and I decided it was just too exhausting for me.

Several days later found me preparing for surgery for Meniere's disease. There was a certain amount of risk involved and as I faced the unknown, I was filled with questions. Would it work? What would the side effects be? It was a private time, interlaced with determination and vulnerability. I was going into the future and stepping out of my boat . . . but in doing so, I knew I was going to lose sight of the shore. Even though I was having recurring vertigo attacks, which were becoming intolerable after twenty years, by having surgery I was giving up what was familiar for what was unfamiliar. What kept me going was a chance for life beyond suffering that would offer a new way of seeing and experiencing the world.

The hardest thing to talk about is how complicated serious risk-taking can be. I found that this is not a place for naïve hope. When I took the aquatic classes, I experienced joy, but also traumatic vulnerability when my body collapsed. Surgery for the disease did not go well and I was left with permanent damage, which even my surgeon can't explain. What happened should not have happened. I took the risk. . . I got out of the boat. Afterwards I felt as if I were nearly drowning, changed forever by taking a risk that did not go as planned. Why did I put all that emotional energy into hoping, daring and risking? Was I a fool?

Despite the disappointment, I don't look at it that way. We need to believe that we can transcend suffering, that resilience of spirit will give us the courage and buoyancy we need to walk on the water which perilously rocks our boats when trouble comes. With the help of God, our friends and family, we can float when we can't touch bottom, pulled safely along within the sacred circle of those we care about and who care about us.

The truth is that we can never avoid uncertainty and fear. This not knowing is part of the journey of hope life calls us to— and it's also what makes us afraid. Yet, we are called to move beyond ourselves, to stretch, to take chances that enable us to live life the best we can. Genuine power comes from embracing our vulnerability, adapting, deepening and believing we can still flourish—even when risks go wrong.

God Who Parts Seas, Walks on Water and Stills Mighty Oceans, thank you for guarding our lives with vigilance, never leaving your post for a moment. You honor and carry our fears so we don't have to. . . always encouraging us to move on to lives of empowerment.

He Said

It was 1985, and my fiancée and I were saving money for our wedding the following year. During this time, I was very active in civic affairs and I found attending neighborhood meetings and community events enjoyable and a way to give back. With city council elections coming up, I decided to take my neighborhood activism to a new level, take a risk and file for public office. I recall thinking "what better place to be if one wanted to really make a difference." But first I needed the support of my wife-to-be as well as her agreement to deplete our wedding savings to get the campaign off the ground and her blessing to quit my job and campaign full time. She offered her full support even promising to vote for me. All right, I had at least two votes. The race was on.

The risk venture had many positive byproducts during the year-long campaign. Family pulled together, our friends learned about campaigning and we met many new friends. With the November election the campaign was over and so was my political career—at that point—I had lost to the incumbent by 123 of the 5,000 votes cast. Had it been worth the risk? Absolutely. Our grassroots campaign exposed new people to politics and taught them to take a risk, to challenge the status quo. Even in losing, it was a tremendous opportunity to participate in democracy, a process most people only criticize from the comfort of their sofa. God challenges us to act and blesses us with individual talents to use, all the while remaining with us, especially when we step out and take risks.

—JPB

She Said

"Can I do it?" I wondered aloud. After being out of the workforce for nine years, did I have the gumption to go back to an 8-5 job? Circumstances had changed in our family and I had to become the breadwinner. What would I do? How could I cope? Would my family fall apart? So many questions and very few answers. Indecisive by nature, instead of fretting, I surrendered to God just as we had during our previous trials and tribulations.

Then a miraculous thing happened: God sent angels. I got a call from my old boss needing someone to start immediately . . . no benefits but good pay. I started that very same week. I also received a call from a teacher at my son's former school and asked her if they had any openings. They did . . . health benefits but less pay. Not having written a resume for 20 years, I found God at the keyboard with me as I keyed in my skills which were compatible for these jobs. Incredibly, I was offered both jobs, and accepted both part time, giving me a chance to decide over time. I chose the one which better suited my creativity and need for purpose, even though it paid much less. Oh Jesus, walker on water, if I just keep my eyes on you, I will stay afloat even in stormy, turbulent times.

—SGB

Work Book Page

Discussion or Journal Questions

1. Adolfo Quezada writes of harrowing times, "We begin, not by strategizing but by surrendering. If you are drowning, go ahead and drown. Be submerged in life in its totality. Remember that water is spiritual." Risk-taking involves submerging ourselves in fearful situations with trust. We say, "Ok, this is too big and too hard for me to figure out."

   Talk about a time when you experienced empowerment by praying like this. Talk about a time when, through hindsight, you can see that your fearful state became a source of wasted energy that was actually detrimental.

2. If we are ever going to be able to become mature risk-takers, we have to learn to be comfortable with hearing the word "No." What are some risks you never took because you let the fear of rejection stop you? Fear of being emotionally exposed or embarrassed when we don't have it all together is another reason why people are reluctant to take risks. Explore any areas where shame is holding you back from living a progressive life.

Goal

To learn not to view fear as an enemy and to explore its presence in relationship to taking positive risks.

Task

Read John 14:22-36. Reflect upon the following four things: (1) the initial confidence Peter had in risk-taking, (2) his sinking once fear took hold, (3) Jesus immediately responding to Peter's cry, "Save me" and (4) the words of Jesus calling us not to doubt. What messages do these passages personally offer you?

Prayer Image

The life and death of Martin Luther King Jr.

Affirmation Statement

I will respect uncertainty and fear of the unknown as I move forward to a bold life that stretches my faith and rewards my efforts.

24

⟶ The Final Lesson: ⟵
Do It with Love

He sustained him in a desert land, in a howling
wilderness waste;
He shielded him, cared for him, guarded him
as the apple of his eye.

—Deuteronomy 32:10

WHEN I came out of the anesthesia following surgery for Meniere's disease a number of years ago, the first thing I noticed was that my vision was severely distorted. Feeling like I'd been hit by a truck, I hesitantly whispered to a nurse, "I can't see . . . " As through a fog, I sensed alarm in my family and in the nurses and doctors coming in and out of my room. "We're walking the floor over you," my surgeon said. These words (though I didn't know it at the time) ushered in a pivotal point in time that would officially begin my evolution from being a caretaker for my family to becoming a care receiver. When I was finally able to return home, even though I couldn't see very well and could barely walk, I could sense our three young son's shock when they saw me. It didn't take a rocket scientist to know they were thinking, *Where is my mother?* Half my face was permanently paralyzed, appearing as if it were melted. To relieve the worry, we all had a genuine, much-needed (albeit cautious) chuckle when the boys said I looked like The Joker from the movie, *Batman.*

Through the years, there have been a lot of disappointments for my family as I continued to decline, as well as many lessons learned and a lot of forgiveness. However, there has also been much maturity and generosity gained, patience mastered and deepened love that weathered very tough times. Many people have experienced this same transition. My friend, Ann Poplawski (who has suffered from disabling chronic illnesses for over twenty years) poignantly describes the process from being a caretaker to becoming a care receiver, "The hardest part of being a care receiver for me is that I feel like a caged bird that wants to fly, spread her wings and experience so many things in life. I want to do for others and I become frustrated with my needing help, because I feel I was born to *give* help!" These words resonate with the perspective offered by Dr. Richard Johnson in his June 2002 Association for Lifelong Adult Ministry newsletter (ALAM), "Each of us needs a ministry all the days of our life, yet when we're sick it's more than hard to continue whatever ministry (love work) formerly filled us. When we're sick we feel that taking care of sickness is our only 'business.' Yet when we're sick, and especially if our sickness becomes chronic, we require, perhaps more than ever, a sustaining ministry."

One of the most valuable things I have discovered as a disabled person learning to be a care receiver is to accept it from my family in the capacity that they are able to give it, and to respect their limitations and boundaries. Emotionally, they might not like to have a long talk on how I'm feeling, but would rather help in a practical way. Ann also writes about this in her life, "I have accepted the care I need and receive from my husband and loved ones, because in doing so, I have seen the beautiful spiritual growth, maturity and blessings that they have received by being a caregiver to me. I have come to see the face of Christ in their faces."

For my friends and thousands like us, on days when chronic illness brings weariness beyond words, blunted senses, inability to do for ourselves and clouded thought processes, we relate to the pain of the world only too well; we understand what it is like to be in the trenches and to consequently grow in authentic empathy. This is where we learn that beyond giving and receiving lies *the gift of spiritual presence* to a hurting world . . . and in that revelation comes the clarity of what is worthwhile in life.

Ann writes, "Being a chronically ill person is a life-changing experience. It is a never-ending process of learning how to accept love and care from others and yet to somehow still keep my dignity and self-respect for my own unique abilities and the things that I alone can offer. In the end, that is the final lesson of receiving care and giving care . . . *you must just do it with love and because of love.*" As I reflect upon Ann's words, I understand what she means. To suffer is fierce. To cope with and release feelings of being a burden requires courage, discipline and strength of character. To channel and extend limited energy positively with mature openness to whatever each day holds is always possible through the fortitude of faith.

> *God Who Cherishes Every Opportunity to Encourage Us, your instruction in how to live the gospel message can be summed up in two phrases: fidelity to the task and committed devotion to our loved ones.*

He Said

Where did it come from? How does she do it? To this day, I still don't know. Our family lives in a very diverse neighborhood only a few minutes from the city's busy downtown. Our neighborhood holds regular meetings, potlucks, barbecues, clean-ups, holiday lighting contests, garage sales, all which make and keep our community vibrant and safe. As is often the case, the creativity and energy in such activity falls on the laps of only a few, sometimes only one. Meet Joyce, 68 years of age, bursting with energy, zest for life, a constant smile and a love for urban life accented with flowers, flowers, and more flowers. If there is any activity fostering a stronger sense of community, Joyce is involved. Although never married, Joyce has more children than the "Old Woman in the Shoe," and she's much kinder too. Any child who lives in our "village" is a child of Joyce's. She opens her flower gardens and bucolic backyard for children's parties that last the whole day. Last year marked her 21st annual summer party!

No, I will never understand Joyce's energy or her everlasting smile. You see, Joyce lives in a wheelchair and has physically suffered from rheumatoid arthritis since childhood. Never has Joyce let her physical handicap confine her indomitable spirit. For 45 years, Joyce was the director of the Courage Cards and Gifts Department at the Courage Center, leading the effort to address rehabilitation and mobility concerns for wheelchair users. For all those years, Joyce's day wasn't over when she returned home from work, a day that began well before sunrise in order for her to catch a ride to work with a colleague or Metro Mobility. Her evenings involved neighborhood meetings, volunteer service on boards and committees, and an active role in local politics. No doubt, there were many days Joyce was tired and hurting, but she pressed forward with courage. Joyce has taught me that courage is a lot like faith. . . the more you exercise it, the stronger it gets. Joyce is an incredible conduit of love, a remarkable woman of courage.

—*JPB*

She Said

Listening has the word "list" in it and I grew up with a dad who thought we could read his mind. At times, it was very frustrating, but it actually has helped my siblings and me tune into the unspoken as well as the spoken word. We learned the art of what wasn't being said and observed what he was really wanting and needing. We also learned that the hardest thing in the world is dependency, especially in our world that fanfares self-sufficiency, going it alone and being tough. The worst feeling is being a burden. Conversely, we are not a burden if we know how to receive. And this is a lost art.

After 44 years, I learned to ask for help and to receive it. I told my family that I was not excited about Christmas, was not feeling up to it because my husband was in prison and unable to be with us. Because it was my turn to host it, I called my sisters and asked them to pitch in. For the meal, I cooked nothing. I ordered KFC chicken and pies and asked my siblings to bring the extras. I also sheepishly asked my brother to fix some things around the house and since he had the same mind-reading upbringing as me, I only had to ask once and they were done! I have to admit my pride suffered briefly, but now I have given up on being "superwoman, go it alone." That didn't serve me, it just made me angry and tired. Asking for help is one of the greatest gifts we can give ourselves or each other, for without understanding how to receive, never can we truly experience the mercy, love and forgiveness that the Lord has waiting for us.   —*SGB*

Work Book Page

Discussion or Journal Questions

1. One thing we need to recognize is that there will never be perfection in caregiving. This very human quality is what gives power and substance to our commitment to one another. Is there someone in your life who needs your rededication as a friend, mate, helper, parent or caregiver? As a care receiver, is there someone you need to stop taking for granted?

2. Redemptive suffering is a beautiful, long-standing Catholic tradition. To feel that the suffering we experience can be offered up for the needs of someone else can bring a sense of empowerment that only faith can provide. Feeling our suffering is of no consequence to anyone or to God isolates and brings the deepest loneliness a person can experience.

   Who are you dependent upon and who is dependent upon you?

Goal

To explore the dynamics of dependency between being a caretaker and a care receiver.

Task

Sometimes, all it takes is a bit of enlightenment to help us reframe attitudes which hurt us and hurt those entrusted to our care. Looking at your list of people who are dependent upon you, ask yourself the following question: Do you unconsciously view them as "chores" or "an honor to be there for?" How do you think you are viewed in light of these two labels?

Prayer Image

The Good Samaritan.

Affirmation Statement

I will always remember that the most empowering spiritual perspectives regarding personal independence teach us that we are inherently created to need one another during times of suffering and trouble.

~ 25 ~

The Shadow of Depression: A Great Teacher

. . . our days on the earth are like a shadow,
. . . in the uprightness of my heart I have freely offered
all these things. —1 Chronicles 29:15b, 17b

A NUMBER of years ago on New Year's Eve, a friend and I each selected a card from a deck of Soul Work cards. The one I drew depicted an image of a woman with her back to the world. It was puzzling to me at the time, but through hindsight, I can see that there was a prophetic element of things to come; shadowlands that came into being following the diminishment of my health, physical appearance and loss of a beloved child, all when I was in my forties and a marital separation when I was fifty-one.

Theologians teach that a soulful life is never without shadow and that some of the soul's power comes from the depths of its shadow qualities. For a long time I tried to keep a particular shadow that is a part of me (and all human beings) at arm's length. Saying the words, "I am depressed," giving it definition, validation and the attention it deserves always stuck in my throat. Because of the stigma attached to it—learning that it must be hidden and not talked about or acknowledged—left an unconscious indelible imprint upon me: that it is bad and shameful to be depressed.

Finally, the day came when I said the words aloud to a friend, *"I am depressed."* Then, I quickly added, *"Don't tell anyone!"* I'd learned to hide it so well—sounding cheerful on the phone to family when I felt anything but cheerful, using exclamation points and an upbeat language in my emails and on my website was easy. No one ever knew when I was feeling down or struggling with suffering. I became a master at hiding it. It takes a lot of energy to cope with depression, sadness, grief or betrayal. My thinking was that if I let on that I was having a challenging day, others would reach out to me, and it would take *more* energy to have to respond—energy that for many reasons, I did not have.

Yet, as I began taking baby steps by allowing myself to stand with my back to the outer world as in the New Year's Eve Soul Work card and admitting to my inner shadow world that I was depressed, I began to have subtle feelings of freedom. It was as if I had crossed a bridge within to be able to acknowledge it. It was a vulnerable admission, to be sure, but by taking my mask off I learned how connected, universal and holy all emotions are. Depression is one of the many faces of the soul and when we hide it—or any emotions that need to be acknowledged—we can't be present to others. As a result, intimacy and authenticity are lost.

This was one of the most powerful lessons I learned and must keep re-learning. Having written four books in about that many years, establishing three websites and writing three columns for various publications enmeshed me in ministry work, all following the death of my son in 1999. People would say to me, "I don't know how you do it . . . " I would just pause and keep going—yet there were days when I felt as if I could not go on with the work and that I felt I would collapse if I had to reach out to one more person. Finally, I had to admit that I had to take care of me; I was depressed and needed to find empowerment for my outreach work from a place of stillness, healing and peace. How could I authentically help others who were depressed when I could not admit that

I was depressed myself? How could I be a wounded healer when I did not attend to my own wounds?

By finding the courage to routinely turn our backs to our outer world and look into our shadowlands, we give ourselves a gift of balance. I found that by acknowledging times of depression or sadness, allowing it to be felt, finding the avenues of comfort I needed and not denying it, gave it a voice. I value that voice beyond measure and it has taught me things that no other teacher could. I also make sure I remember the words of a wise friend who said that whenever it is possible to prevent or alleviate suffering, we are compelled by love to do so. It is especially hard but truly necessary to do this for ourselves. It is only when it is apparent that resistance will not help, that we enter into it and transform it into a life-giving force.

> *God of Dark Nights of the Soul, men and women of empowerment know the truth deep in their hearts— being spiritual does not mean that we dwell only in the land of positive thinking. Depression is not a sign of weakness or lack of faith; it is a language of the soul that must be attended to, embraced and allowed to speak.*

He Said

She was creative, bright, energetic and beautiful. That was my sister Jan. She married young and had four beautiful children whom she fussed over as a stay-at-home mom. After a divorce, she immersed herself in the workforce and although she hadn't been in the workplace for many years, Jan climbed the ladder at lightening speed. Jan showed a cheerful image and managed on little sleep. When we saw her at family events, she was always smiling, appearing joyful. But something was wrong. She called my house often because she had a sincere fondness for our infant son who, by the time he was two years old, was able to tell us the name of his favorite auntie. Slowly we began to realize she had a drinking problem. Now in her mid-forties after splitting with someone she loved and losing her job, she began drinking more.

Jan called me at my office on a Wednesday afternoon and said she was bored and maybe it was time she went to see Aunt Stella. Aunt Stella was my mother's sister who thirty years earlier had taken her own life. I couldn't believe it. I didn't want to accept that she was talking this way. For the first time in her life, Jan admitted she was depressed. After we talked for awhile she seemed better, and I told her I had to catch a plane in the morning but would come see her on Saturday as soon as I got back. The next day after checking into my hotel, I received an emergency message. Something was wrong. I called my wife and she quietly said, "Joe, Jan is dead."

So many depressed people try to self-medicate using alcohol. Jan's remedy had finally killed her. I felt I had failed her; that we all had failed her. What happened? I believed that depression only affected other people, not my beautiful, bubbly sister with four incredible children, the youngest only 12. How wrong I was.

—*JPB*

She Said

In 1994, I gave birth to a long-awaited child and although it was my choice to stay home I had no idea how difficult this would be after being in the workforce for 17 years without a break. Not being a "working woman" I had lost my identity. Two years later, my father-in-law and father died within two months of each other. I was so miserable that I got up the nerve one day to call the Employee Assistance Program through my husband's work. On top of being depressed, I was angry at myself that I just couldn't "snap out of it." I was referred to a therapist who lived nearby and who was very kind and empathetic. With her help and by starting an exercise program, I felt better and was able to enjoy life again.

In 2002 when my husband's legal troubles began and our world turned upside down, my mood took a nosedive and I knew I would need more than therapy sessions and exercise. I could barely get myself out of bed and each step I took felt as if I was submerged in cement. My doctor prescribed an anti-depressant and within weeks, my mood swings leveled and I was in a steady emotional state which allowed me to cope.

While depression remains a stigma in our society, it is as common as any physical illness and can be caused by a chemical imbalance in the brain. God will help us, but it is our job to help Him help us. And those of us who have benefited from antidepressants must ensure that this medicine is available to all people who need it, not just those who can afford it—by opening up, speaking about it and reassuring others its OK.   *—SGB*

Work Book Page

Discussion or Journal Questions

1. Dr. Robert Thompson teaches that it is important to understand the distinctions between sadness, which requires assimilation, the sharing of hope with others and feeling their support, and depression, which is a sickness that requires acknowledgment, classification, treatment and supervision.

    Looking back, can you see distinctions between the two? If you never gave the sadness or depression you experienced a voice, allow it to speak to you now; write down what comes to mind, expressing the pain you felt and images that described it.

2. Some of the finest theologians, musicians, composers and literary geniuses experienced times of depression—yet through the experience, offered works of great depth and beauty to the world. How do you explain the spiritual language of depression translating to such expressive creativity? Talk about times and ways you have brought something to light out of a time of depression or sadness.

Goal

To learn to respect all seasons of the soul and to give depression the voice, education and support it deserves.

Task

In *Reflections in the Light,* Shakti Gawain wrote that we all have a spiritual trap door that we fall through, into the bright world of our spirits, when we expect to hit bottom. If you were to draw a trap door and depict the hopes and dreams you envision awaiting you, what would they be? Once you give specific language to your aspirations, it is not wishful thinking that will bring them into being but setting realistic goals, making specific plans and finding the support you need to usher in the necessary sacred momentum.

Prayer Image

A cradle.

Affirmation Statement

As an authentic spiritual being, I will no longer deny, feel shame about or pretend I am not sad or depressed when I am.

~ 26 ~

—✦ Telling Our Stories: ✦— Voices We Carry

... our ancestors have told us, what deeds you performed in their days, in the days of old: and the light of your countenance, for you delighted in them.

—Psalm 44:1b,3b

STORYTELLING involves the specific act of joining or relating to others in order to provide a sense of union or belonging. These connections are crucial. Bible stories, for example, carry messages of our own personal experiences. Through them, we are reminded that growth is always a choice and as the biblical person's story comes alive to us, we are inspired to envision the empowered lives we are called to.

Honoring and connecting with the memories and stories of our kinsmen and women who have gone before us is often an overlooked source of comfort and inspiration. Sometimes, we forget about our great grandparents, great aunts, uncles and other relatives who have passed over into the mysterious realm of the spirit. Through faith and scripture we know that someday we will be welcomed by our ancestors who have lived lives of courage, experience and wisdom. 1 Corinthians 13:12 promises this, "For now, we see in a mirror dimly, but then we will see face to face."

Have you ever laid awake at night and wondered who will come after you? Do you ever feel a tenderness and need to protect your family and friends, knowing that the world is in chaos, besieged by war and famine; suffering from materialism, violence and ecological atrocities? Do you wish your voice and life stories could reach through time, gathering in those who will be your descendants? If you do, you are entering a sacred phase of caring and connection that comes from being tapped into the deepest realms of God. When I look in my great-grandmother's mirror and see my own image, I wonder if someday a great grandchild looking in the same mirror will wonder about me and want to know the stories of my life, as I do of my ancestors'.

"The faith and the hope of our ancestors, acknowledged or not, is also within us; we persevere on its momentum. We must learn to lean on these ancestors to the extent that they are solid, and to trust in the truth as we have received and understand it," writes Larry Woiwode in *Inheriting the Land.* This brings to mind a photo I have of my mother, Lois and my four aunts, Dorothy, Eleanore, Marilyn and Peggy— the five sisters leaning against a white, wooden railing. I cherish the photo because it invites me to remember the stories of their lives and provides a timeless connection to the happiness and love captured on their faces.

One night long ago, I passed by our youngest son, Mic's bedroom door on my way to get a drink of water. "Mom . . . mom . . ." I could hear his small voice calling out through the darkness. "Come and sit on my bed, I can't sleep," he said. I groped my way across his cluttered bedroom to the foot of the bed. Tossing me a pillow, he said, "let's talk awhile." I was sleepy but fought off the urge to creep back to my own bed. At thirteen, Mic was entering that age of independence and I was sharply aware of the fact that midnight chats with him had gotten few and far between. I was somewhat taken aback when he said, "I can't quit thinking about the world."

"What do you mean?" I asked.

"I can't understand why the world has to have mean people who murder others," he said, "and who kidnap kids. People aren't even safe in their own homes in big cities. The world seems so scary, I keep wondering what it will be like by the time I've grown up." He paused and then, with the endearing but unrealistic dreams of a child said, "I want to build a log cabin across the creek from you and Dad and live here forever."

I remember smiling gently to myself because our son was not voicing anything that I had not pondered myself during the deep thinking hours of the night. The world seemed kind of scary to me, too. Safe within the warm darkness of my son's little room, we talked—about life, our family's faith, our beliefs and all the good things that have shaped us through the years. We took turns telling each other stories and memories of the ways we each felt we had experienced God in personal ways. Mic surprised me with the poignant thoughts he shared. I could tell that some of the stories I shared surprised him, too, and I could sense him grinning in the dark. That night we learned things about each other that we didn't know before.

Connecting our deepest fears with the times we had felt God's care caused the scary thoughts and questions to fade. As Mic drifted back into a peaceful sleep, I tucked his favorite stuffed dinosaur under his chin. Now, many years later, following his death in 1999, in one of life's greatest mysteries, I carry his beloved voice within—as does my family and Mic's close friends. We keep his beloved memory alive through the stories we tell of who he was. This remains one of the most sacred connections in my life and I am grateful that the reverence that was instilled in me by my parents and grandparents lives on as a legacy of spiritual, eternal connection that will never be severed. As Macrina Wiederkehr writes in *Behold Your Life: A Pilgrimage Through Your Memories,* "Every person who ever lived upon this earth is still here. Their bodies have returned to the earth. Their spirits, too, in some mysterious and incomprehensible manner, linger in the land. Heaven and earth touch."

> *God Who Weaves Consolation Through the Stories of Our Lives, you are the thread that connects the pages of our past, present and future. Comfort us through our kinsfolk, love us through our soulmates and family and enfold us through our friends.*

He Said

Someone once told me you have to know where you've been to know where you're going. It was her way of encouraging me to learn my family history. I was embarrassed to admit I didn't know much about my history except that my grandparents had migrated to America from Poland in search of a better life. They died when I was young and my father wasn't fond enough of the "old days" to talk about them. Luckily my Great Uncle Mike was a walking history book who in his 90's lived independently, enjoyed long walks and longed for company. Twice a week, we would sit at the kitchen table of his tiny house talking about my family's history while consuming the drink he swore was key to his longevity: cranberry juice diluted with tap water. Our talks continued through my high school years and Great Uncle Mike was the subject of one of my very first college history papers. In addition to family history, he also instilled in me an array of positive values that today I teach my son.

At 98, Great Uncle Mike came to live with us, continuing to enlighten us about a past we never knew. He lived to be 99—and many remarked how unfortunate it was he didn't reach 100, a regret quickly discounted by the priest presiding at his funeral who reminded everyone that, counting his time in the womb, he did in fact reach 100. Uncle Mike had so much to share; he just needed others to take the time to honor his human connection to the past. There isn't a day that goes by when I don't think of Great Uncle Mike as I begin it with a glass of cranberry juice diluted with water. Maybe I'll be the one to make it to 100!   —*JPB*

She Said

Growing up in a small town in Minnesota, we were webbed together in a most miraculous way—on my mom's side, we had Grandpa and his single son Uncle Chuck up the street, Uncle Tony and Aunt Esther diagonally across from us, Aunt Gert and Uncle Lawrence a block away, and Uncle Joe and Aunt Max on the other side of town 50 yards away. On my dad's side, was Great Aunt Angie who ran the only café in town, his second cousin Leo and wife Leona who ran the only grocery store in town and Grandpa two miles away on his farm who visited us each and every day. We not only felt connected, but we felt protected by the whole town.

The silk spinnings of this web were strong and resilient given the ardent Catholic faith each of these men and women shared. My mom's great grandfather had been active in helping build the church and had donated the land for the cemetery (interestingly, he was also the first one buried there). My dad's father had home-steaded some land in Montana and donated the altar for the church in Sunburst. All of the above mentioned kin sacrificed to build a new church during my youth. Uncle Tony also donated the large statue of the Blessed Virgin, and my mom donated a smaller statue of Mary in memory of my dad when he died.

Never would any of my kin ever consider missing church on Sunday. My mother's word to us when we toyed with the idea of skipping church would be to remind us of Jesus in the Garden of Gethsemane when he approached the sleeping apostles, "Could you not even spend an hour with me?" We are connected to Jesus, to each other and to all generations in a timeless bond of faith.

—*SGB*

Work Book Page

Discussion or Journal Questions

1. When Mic and I were sharing stories, he told me of a time he had felt closest to God. One morning he had gone to Daub's Lake to camp out and wait for duck hunting season to open. As he watched the sun rise over the glassy lake, it was as if the world came alive in those first golden moments. I could sense his soul fill with awe, joy and vitality as he remembered that sacred experience. I reverently carry his story and it comforts me. What are some stories you carry of loved ones who have passed on?

2. Joseph Campbell wrote that when we look back over our lifetime, it can seem to have had a consistent order and plan, as though composed by a divine novelist, with each experience structuring the next. Do you experience the stories in your life as having a divine link when viewed through the perspective of faith? Research your family tree if you've never done so.

Goal

To explore the deep value, honor and privilege of telling our own stories and carrying those of others in our hearts as a sacred connection between this world and the next.

Task

Campbell also teaches that the reason we all need to tell and understand our stories is because they offer passages into our search for truth and significance. If you were to write an autobiography of your life, what would you entitle it? Have you ever thought of the creative power of the Holy Spirit being the life in your stories, lovingly calling, "Tell me more, tell me everything, leave nothing out, I want to hear every precious facet of your life—and I want you to listen to my stories and lessons woven into yours."

Prayer Image

Loved ones sitting around a campfire roasting marshmallows.

Affirmation Statement

With great awe, I acknowledge that I am a divine point between heaven and earth—a living connection that carries my deceased loved ones' stories within my own until I join them in heaven.

—➤❊ Of Priceless Value: ❊◀— Unblocking Soul Work

I will give them one heart, and put a new spirit within them;
I will remove the heart of stone. . . and give them a heart of
flesh,   —Ezekiel 11:19

I RECENTLY read an essay by Sr. Joan Chittister in which she described life as an epic of challenges meant to be withstood; a sequence of stumblings from which we are meant to evolve; a series of circular lessons meant to be drained of every glory that wisdom has to offer.

These words remind me of a fairy tale that I wrote in the summer of 1991. "Life Beyond the Mirror" is about a princess who was disenchanted by life, searching for meaning and filled with a longing she couldn't explain. It begins, "She stood before the mirror, a caricature, she felt, of the young woman she had once been. Her eyes etched with sorrow, she viewed the sagging flesh, silver-streaked hair, thickening waistline, wrinkled neck. 'You are not me,' she said to the stranger in the mirror, 'you are not me!' " In my story, the princess then smashes the mirror with a fire poker, its shards falling amongst her disheveled heap of finery. The story then descends into gloomy pages that basically go nowhere. I wanted this story to be beautiful, and I invested every drop of wisdom that I had in it, stretching myself and digging as deeply as I could into my psyche. I wanted it to be a spiritual masterpiece but it ended up being a flat, morose embarrassment with false optimism throughout that reflected old black and white preconceptions that were not working for me personally or in the story.

For over a decade the story was stuffed into the back of my files, until I finally threw it into the trash. I felt it represented such a waste of my time and energy and—since it lacked the depth I had hoped for—that it was useless. Days later I salvaged it, and I decided to do some soul work and see what it was *really* about. In the story, the princess finds a diary that was written by her now deceased father, the king, when she was a child. The diary ends with an entry by her beloved father about a trip he was about to take with his most trusted friend, Zaimes, during which there was a tragic hunting accident in which her father died.

The rest of the story is about the princess's long journey as an adult to find meaning in life as she earnestly searches for answers to questions she can't articulate. Finally, a slim passage reveals a stronghold, "The vulnerable one within her who was really quite ordinary in the sacred sense of the word . . . who had nothing to offer but inner growth, service and roots beckoned. What a woman! What power she held! What significance!" The princess realized that she had been seeking wisdom for wisdom's sake alone, which had left her enlightened but cold and empty. In the end, with unconditional care, patience and mentoring from a wise guide, her heart of stone becomes a living heart that reveres life, God and other people. Wisdom then flows naturally—as it is supposed to—out of the comfort of coming to terms with losing her father. With this healing in place, devotion to God and others flows as she becomes her true highest self, unblocked by grief and disillusionment.

The final passage concludes with unexpected beauty as the princess says, "Then, we must make a toast!" Handing a pewter chalice filled with rich, sweet wine to the monk who had been her mentor, she pronounces, "To memorable living!" Lifting his cup he salutes her, "Yes, to a lifetime of memorable loving, giving and growing." Then, *"Your father would be proud of you."* Her response is caught on the wind as he canters off, but not before an intense look of kinship passes between them.

"Your father would be proud of you." I finally understood that the whole story was about processing the longing for my beloved dad who had died fifteen years before and realizing with profound joy that he is proud of me. As I understood, I thought, "My God, the power of soul work. What value, what priceless value."

God Who Orchestrates Our Creativity, thank you for reminding us that soul work is never about the quality being judged as good or bad or black or white—but about the transforming, comforting glory of its power to transform and heal us through seasons of stumbling.

He Said

Steve, a 40-year-old farmer from Wisconsin, is blessed with a smile that could warm the soul of the world's grumpiest person. He loves the Lord. He greets people with an outstretched hand, never fails to say "hello" to everyone he passes and engages in sincere discussions with those to whom he's grown close. After years of studying the Bible, Steve became a positive influence in the lives of many as a result of his knowledge of scripture.

When I was experiencing great adversity in my life, I went to see Steve. Together we studied The Word and reflected on its meaning. We met frequently and he helped me commit myself to pursuing an internal peace that only The Word could provide. After two months, I excitedly told Steve that I was feeling closer to God every day. He responded with his familiar smile and twinkling eyes, "Just think how close you will be to Him two months from now!" He's right. We are all on a journey. For some people, it may seem as if they depart and return to the very same station, their journey flat and uneventful. For others, their train keeps climbing, taking them to new places, new heights, meeting people along the way who make their journey more fruitful. This latter train is the one filled with passengers whose open hearts invite the Lord to fill their journey to the brim. And the more fulfilled, the more they are able to share their overflow with others. All aboard!   —*JPB*

She Said

"You may not need it now, but you will someday," my mother declared to my grown brothers who were not regular churchgoers. My mother equated going to church with having faith and being able to turn to God in your time of need. I did not really buy her reasoning at the time and would roll my eyes as I heard this lecture again and again over the years.

Then, for the first time in our lives my husband and I found ourselves in a situation that was totally beyond our control. There was nothing we could do except let those in power decide our fate. Able only to discuss this legal matter with our attorney, we turned to God for answers, help and guidance. We began by praying the prayers we had learned as children. I also taught my husband the rosary and then branched out to other prayers, to Padre Pio and the Divine Mercy. Simultaneously, we joined a bible study, were prayed over and welcomed the Holy Spirit into our hearts. Realizing the gift of tongues was a special language between God and us helped us in the darkest moments when words were inadequate. It was a unique freedom to express what was in our souls. And for the first time in our lives, we began to understand that the Catholic Mass was not only *ritual* but *spiritual,* an experience where we could feel the glory of God the Father, the humanness of Christ the son, and the forgiveness of the Holy Spirit. I now understand why Mom thought going to church was so important. It was our chance to get close to God and share His love and our love with others simultaneously. —*SGB*

Work Book Page

1. When is the last time anyone said they were proud of you? When is the last time you told anyone you were proud of them? When is the last time you told *yourself* that you are proud of yourself?

2. When my potted narcissus bulbs finished blooming and it was time to remove the bulbs from the pot, I was shocked to see how rootbound they were. They were jammed in so tightly, that I had to take a knife and cut them apart. When we have spiritual blocks in our lives, we don't realize how intertwined this phenomena becomes to our daily lives above the surface. The block can cause us to feel rootbound without even knowing why we feel that way. In the story of the princess, as she found true wisdom, she found the value of a healthy life rooted in faith.

Talk about the difference between being rootbound by blocks in your life and what you would like to be rooted in.

Goal

To explore, recognize and heal hurtful memories or grief that are blocking the flow of creativity, faith and joyful living.

Task

When I was a child, after a rain storm, the driveway in front of our house would get very muddy and nearly impassable. Pools of water would settle in pockets everywhere and then the fun would begin. We would all go out with big sticks to make ditches to drain the water from the road. I remember how my mother would get nearly stuck in the soupy mess as the mud made sucking sounds each time she pulled her foot out—as if it were reluctant to let her go. We thought this was an adventure and I remember a lot of laughing. Mother was the Master Ditcher and we children her small, eager apprentices. Through this special memory, I am reminded that when psychologically we have emotional blocks that need ditching, it doesn't have to be all gloom and doom. With the help and support of others, it can actually be a rewarding experience.

It is good to remind ourselves from time to time that with a little spiritual poking and ditching, we can free ourselves from that which sucks us down—and find our life path looking better than ever. Sometimes people say they feel drained of strength and vitality by life's obstacles. However, we can drain the obstacle of its power to have a hold on us through prayer, rest, loving support, goal setting, life-style changes and optimism.

Talk about avenues you have not given a serious chance, that could help you break through a problem that blocks your happiness. Do you have an empowering childhood memory that could offer you a new perspective for an old problem?

Prayer Image

A geyser.

Affirmation Statement

I will not run from obstacles or unresolved pain that block my spiritual progress in life, but rather will discover, heal and free the memories that hold me back.

~ 28 ~

⟶✺ Living the Miracle: ✺⟵
Thoughts on Recovery

*Did you experience so much for nothing?—if it really
was for nothing.
Well, then, does God supply you with the Spirit and
work miracles among you . . . by your believing what
you heard?*—Galatians 3:4, 5

THE pivotal month of March—it comes in like a lion and goes out like a lamb, so the saying goes. It is a messy, paradoxical month to be sure. Outside my apartment, there were ten-foot high piles of dirty, melting snow and rivulets of water trickling down the street everywhere, and gushing off the eaves of the nearby grocery store. Some days it was extremely foggy out and you couldn't discern where the sky ended and the frozen lake began. On the television news, the prediction of an encroaching snow storm added to the unstable, diverse weather.

I'd never seen a frozen lake thaw and when I asked a clerk at the drug store if the lakes would open early, he got a light in his eye when he said he was sure of it. What would it be like, I wondered in anticipation. At the moment, there was only slush and standing water on top of ice. As I thought of my life journey and the many stages of recovery I had experienced in the last year, I mused how—like the month of March—we all have stormy, moody, slushy seasons of uncertainty and upheaval.

It was while I was processing an especially deep concern and in the midst of mending that a thought came into my mind with such

176

176

clarity, it took me aback: "*You are living the miracle of recovery.*" Every day, for weeks, the thought would be there—reminding me that recovery is about restoration, reawakening and resurrection— one step at a time.

As a friend and I were driving around the lakes eating ice cream cones, we could see for miles. The black fields lay bare, receptive and open for spring planting and we could see that the frozen lakes were already thawing around the edges. In a few places, you could see areas of open, choppy water rippling with the strong March winds, alluring to the returning Canadian geese who gathered by the dozens. You could feel the reawakening spirit of joy in nature and as the sun warmed our faces, the brightness of it glinted off our sunglasses.

My friend and I reviewed and talked about the four Empowering Elements that seemed to be the most important in successful recovery:

1. Being willing to lovingly surrender to that which we couldn't control and not to obsess about outcomes.

2. Being open to taking initiative.

3. Taking risks and trying new things that move us out of our comfort zone.

4. Discerning the truth about our deepest motives—and having the courage to face it and prayerfully live it.

We talked about truths that had been frozen in our hearts and about the hope that was melting the jagged edges of repressed feelings. Sometimes, before the Big Thaw and just before the lakes open up, there is an eerie, mystical creaking sound that can be heard. You can hear it through the night, a subtle, shifting sound that rises and falls. In the morning when you wake up, great sheets of ice lay on the shoreline, moved there by the thaw; while in the lake, chunks of it float in open water.

A miracle is described as a marvel, revelation or wonder. Recovery is described as returning to normal. That March, I realized that living a life of recovery is an ongoing spiritual miracle— and that having the faith to believe in the process should be as normal and natural as the miracle of winter evolving into spring.

> *God Whose Spirit Can Melt the Coldest Hearts, there is no inner weather of the soul that isn't valued, understood and empowered by the miracle of your love.*

He Said

One Sunday morning, our family attended a parish in one of the poorest, high-crime neighborhoods in the city. The dynamic priest had given up a prestigious job as Spiritual Director at St. Thomas University to minister instead to this fledgling inner-city parish. During my first visit, I felt a spiritual stirring and wept halfway through Mass. Puzzled, I came back the following Sunday and again I wept. I was moved deeply by both the love of the parish members and the incredible urgency Father Greg embodied. Here was a rail-thin man who consumed over 100 pills a day just to stay alive. At the same time that he was enduring dialysis and on the national kidney and lung transplant list, he was challenging us to be more, do more, expect more. "Why can't we do more for the troubled youth? Why don't we shut off the televisions and get involved? Why can't we fully open our heart to Jesus and hear His message about loving and helping our neighbor."

Always calling us to service and radical love, Father Greg frequently said "I don't want special concern. I don't want pity. Put that compassion to work saving the neighborhood!" He did not let his illness distract his vision for improving the lives of children in the neighborhood. He used his own suffering to let us know he was human like the rest of us, yet despite setbacks, there was always something we could give, some small miracle of care we could bestow. If a man with cystic fibrosis could accomplish so much, imagine the difference healthy people could make. He let us know that we had run out of excuses and *now* was the time to act.

After much suffering, Father Greg was called home in 2003 at the age of forty-seven—his imprint mighty. His life was a living revelation of faith and empowerment wrought through spiritual recovery, restoration, reawakening and resurrection—in both his miraculous life and ours.   —*JPB*

She Said

Living the miracle of recovery is not always easy . . . occasionally it is going to be painful, gut-wrenching, consciousness-raising and soulful. It is going to be work, because it will mean thawing and stripping layers of an external façade to uncover internal passions that, if you're like me, you've disavowed for years. For me, it started with identifying what I did not want. It required questioning, journaling, and frank, honest excavation to reach my true self. Most of all, it required clearing the noise to hear what was in the silence.

Two books I found especially helpful were *Simple Abundance* and *The Artist's Way: A Course in Discovering and Recovering Your*

Creative Self. The first book helped me understand the need to clear the clutter from my life, while holding on to those things that defined who I was (the things that I innately loved, gravitated towards). The next book got me journaling three pages each morning without editing a thought, sloughing off all extraneous thoughts. Clearing all the physical and spiritual debris from my mind revealed that my true passion was writing—and that this was the gift God meant for me to use as I opened myself to insight, inspiration and guidance. Through my commitment to spiritual recovery the miracle of creative growth opened doors for me that I could never have imagined. *—SGB*

Work Book Page

Discussion or Journal Questions

1. Julia Cameron writes in *The Artist's Way,* "Time and again, I have seen a recovering creative do the footwork of becoming internally clear and focused . . . only to have the universe fling open an unsuspected door. One of the central tasks of creative recovery is learning to accept this generosity." Specifically list hopes and dreams you would like to open through your recovery; visualize it coming true through meditation and prayer.

2. Read and discuss the four Empowering Elements listed in the opening reflection on page 177. Talk about how each is present in your life and list areas where you would like to strengthen one or more of them.

Goal

To explore the dynamics of recovery on the deepest creative and spiritual level.

Task

In Romans 8:18-25, we read that the whole of creation groans with us as we wait patiently for hope. Verses 26 and 27 tell us "that very Spirit intercedes for us with sighs too deep for words. And God, who searches the heart, knows what is the mind of the spirit . . . ." Listen to the weather report and using the terminology of a meteorologist, describe the weather of your heart.

Prayer Image

A weatherman's radar screen.

Affirmation Statement

I will view my recovery as a supportive partnership with God who sees all, knows all—and prepares me ahead of time for anything life can throw at me with the promise of his guiding presence.

~ 29 ~

The Glory That is God: Believe in the Magic

Yours, O Lord, are the greatness, the power, the glory, the victory and the majesty.   —1 Chronicles 29:11a

FOR twenty-eight years, I chronicled the landscape of life in the village where I lived with my family into hundreds of articles and journals dated 1975 to 2003. More often than not, I felt enfolded by a way of life that was filled with hope, promise and adventure at every turn. Though it transpired slowly over time, I witnessed the gradual decline of our little town—until it had nearly died out with only two businesses remaining. I never dreamed this could happen as I wrote, "How can a town die? All those dreams, all that magic . . . where did it go?" People replied with nostalgic resignation, "That's life." I guess it was and is, but the process and noting of these changes was very important to me and I am glad that I recorded my own responses to it. As I did so, I felt as if I were walking the dusty roads in my mind as I imagined buildings and businesses still standing which had been gone for decades. In my imagination, I resurrected people who had long since passed on, as I remembered their voices and laughter, struggles, heartache and transitions.

"It seems like only yesterday that an elderly family friend rode by our house on his lawn mower with a package of cut-up wieners in his pocket to win over our 'wary-of-strangers' dog. It worked every time. I can still see the basketball hoop up at the fire station leaning to the left as a handful of village kids shot baskets—my three sons among them. And over there a small cluster of farmers leaning against the sun-baked brick wall of the grocery store by the pop machine, discussing the latest gossip and politics as the owner of the tiny gas station strode across the street from the café to gas up a honking pick-up truck. Three sweat-streaked men, pals since boyhood, pull up to the tavern for something cold after a long day of cementing—while two women called the Can Pickers by our sons because they collect aluminum pop cans to sell at the salvage yard saunter up to the post office to mail a letter. The 6 o'clock whistle blows, and our dog raises his head like a wolf and howls religiously like he did every day when he heard it. Laughing, I observe our son's black lab puppy emulate our older dog, raising his puppy lips and yowling a kindergarten version of the grown-up dog howl."

Speaking the truth about our lives, the places we've lived and the people we knew is a multi-layered undertaking. There is always a paradox as we face the reality that towns, loved ones and even marriages can decline or die . . . but sometimes they resurrect to go on to become something else. Always there is metamorphosis—yet, on foggy white days, misty evenings when dusk falls, during the silence of a heavy snow fall, or when I walk in the pelting rain under my old black umbrella, there is a subtle sense of time and space overlapping. This is eternity reminding us that in God, the momentum of our lives is seamless, including our temporary, earthly sorrow.

In *Circle of Mysteries: The Women's Rosary Book*, Christin Lore Weber writes, "Sorrow pours out of us when what we love is gone and cannot be brought back because it is changed completely. Sorrow is energy pouring out through what is split in us. It is what is left of what connected us and made us whole. It is blood seeping out. It is what remains of life-as-it-was before a quake surprised us and left us being someone we can't recognize. These are the mysteries of sorrow."

As I processed my marital separation during the summer of 2003, the grief was hard to bear. I realized that sometimes when a life quake comes, it is not always ourselves that we can't recognize but a soul mate. People can change so much that they become like strangers, starting out one way and by the time life gets through with them, ending up completely different than who you thought they were.

As I meditated upon the loss, sorrow, change and new season I found myself thrust into, I wondered how in the world I was going to be able to pick up so many pieces left behind following the fall-out. Then, unexpectedly, something beautiful came to me. I had been working on my "coming of age" young adult novel, *Guardians*. Yet, I felt that an important passage was missing, that wouldn't come through. Finally, after lots of prayers and many false starts, I let go and it just slipped through, in its entirety. The book is auto-biographical fiction, and I am ten years old at the time. I wrote in part:

"Mom Lois had had a talk with her about something girls get, called Time of the Month and Joni was filled with questions. When would it happen to her? What would it be like? Would that mean she had become a woman and couldn't be a girl anymore? Joni felt stricken, amazed and filled with wonder. She began thinking about winter coming…and how one day soon heavy gray skies would surrender to the season and it would begin to snow . . . and snow and snow. Joni loved lifting her face to the snow, letting the flakes catch in her eyelashes and melt on her tongue. She loved viewing the red barn through the veil of white, falling snow—and how it would blur boundaries so you couldn't even see where the road was.

The first snow of the season was always a wonder to Joni, a quiet glory she reveled in, its presence like a silent, haunting humming that was a beautiful language all its own. To her, this was God speaking. This was eternity revealing itself. This was peace. As Joni thought of when her first Time of the Month would come, she knew she would think of snow, red barns and glory. She wondered if she would be transformed as a girl in her new season, like the land was during the first snows. Suddenly Joni realized she had tears running down her cheeks and she quickly wiped them away with the heels of her hands. She jumped up, running down the hill pretending she was a wild horse—instead of a wild girl."

As I thought of what I'd written, I realized that the timeless words were pertinent to my new stage in life as a woman learning to live alone. I was again facing a transforming rite of passage—as life-altering as the wondrous but frightening first time of the month. And like ten-year-old Joni, I felt the deep pang of knowing there would be no going back to what was. Weber refers to life passages such as these as the blood of wisdom beckoning. As I began the healing process in earnest, I painted my beautiful fingernails a deep red—as a ritual commemorating my vow to do the soul work the journey would require and to walk it with God. My temporarily shaken but determined hope echoed Weber's words, "Glory that we can endure. Glory in the gathering of all that's torn, broken, scattered with the wind. Glory when there's nothing left but pain and yet we still go on." I knew instinctively that I wanted that which was split in me healed by the glory that is God, who intimately draws each of us—every man, woman and child—forward to new lives that bless. More than ever, I realized that both this glory and the mystery of sorrow teach us to surrender to the seasons of change with trust and confidence in new beginnings.

As I thought about this, I was reminded of long ago summers when I walked by the rustling, green cornfields along the country roads and detected a hint of subtle, mysterious shifting, as if the very field was alive, breathing and whispering with a thousand voices. Even though I live in a new place now, I realized that decline, loss and moving from one place to another never takes these things from us at all. The familiar language goes way beyond words, the spiritual truth always clear: *Believe in the magic always. It never leaves and always goes with us, merging the old with the new.*

> *God Who fills our Hearts with Eternal Truth, the essence of all that we loved lives on in us—instructing, comforting, challenging and exhorting us to live a life of glory, service and faith.*

He Said

During Adoration of the Blessed Sacrament, a time our church sets aside for quiet prayer, I saw our priest on his knees in the back pew praying fervently and reverently with his hands folded together and his eyes closed. It was as though every fiber of him was wholeheartedly committed to Jesus Christ. He later told me that each day he asks the Lord to make him a man of deeper understanding and holiness. I was so puzzled because here was a priest, a man of God, a highly educated teacher, leader and administrator. Surely he must have reached the ultimate relationship with God long ago? This immature thinking was early on in my own spiritual development when I did not realize that the closer you got to God the more there was to understand.

Today I pray daily for a deeper understanding and closeness with God. I have spiritually matured to realize the more one seeks Him, the more one wants Him. In other words, turning to Him and living your life in obedience to Him brings us closer and closer to Him. I envision God much like the patient fisherman, hooking us, yet giving us slack when we need it, and then slowly reeling us in when we are finished fighting and ready for the path of righteousness. I have a closer relationship with the Lord today, closer than ever before—until tomorrow arrives. Give yourself to Him. Seek Him. Grow with Him. And say yes to Him.   —*JPB*

She Said

One day as I was driving down a comfortable tree-lined street, listening to the radio, a revelation occurred to me. The guest on the radio was recalling a time she was terribly sick and her Daddy asked her what would make her feel better. She said a blue plum. Blue plums were not in season but out of love, he drove all night to get his daughter what she wanted. When she awoke the next morning, her Daddy approached her bed dog-tired, but grinning from ear to ear. Her eyes opened wide as he ushered out a whole bushel of blue plums onto her bed. From that moment on, her recovery was cinched. His demonstration of love began to heal her from the inside out.

The story above crystallized for me what love means—to listen, to be specific and to deliver. The grandeur of the gift has nothing to do with its impact, instead it's how it touches our heart and assures us specifically that we are loved. This past Christmas my son's favorite gift was a kitten, something he had been asking for for three years and the best part about it was that he got to pick the kitten out himself; my favorite gift was a ceramic plate that my husband had made me in prison—he had written my quote about hope on its face; and Joe's favorite gift was one he gave himself— hours and hours of drawing a picture of his son for although he wasn't physically able to be with him, he spent hours in communion with him as he painstakingly drew his beautiful boy and could present it to Josiah for Christmas.

God wants us to experience joy and to help others experience joy. It's as simple as finding out someone's favorite candy bar and giving it to them for no reason at all, much more special than a flashy gift when expected. God is simple; God is love; God is simply love.   —*SGB*

Work Book Page

Discussion or Journal Questions

1. In my book, *Tall in Spirit,* I likened change to the first killing frost of autumn that reveals the backbone of the land. Talk about a change that, as you moved from one way of living, being or thinking to another, brought a gift of revelation you did not expect.

2. Talk about the importance of rituals in your life, especially those that help you feel empowered during difficult times. When I moved to my new home, one of my rituals was to make a sign for my door that said *Casa De Salud,* which in Spanish means house of health or place of healing. Doris, a friend who lives in my building, extended my ritual by calling her apartment *Casa De Salud II.* If you were to make a sign for your door, what would it say?

Goal

To spiritually explore the mystery and synergy between good-byes in life and new beginnings.

Task

Talk about hellos in your life that have followed farewells. For me, some of these included making new friends, experiencing a beautiful new church, a deeper bond with my children, brothers and sisters, learning the language of a completely new geography and spirit of place, and discovering that I am stronger than I thought I was. Even the dedication I have for my ministry work and writing experienced a "hello again" with a resurgence of passion.

What are some examples from your life?

Prayer Image

Passengers waving goodbye and throwing confetti as a ship leaves harbor.

Affirmation Statement

I will remember that the glory of new beginnings always follows the end of something forgiven, transformed, grieved and sacredly bid farewell to.

━━◈ The Glory of Stillness: ◈━━
What Must Come First

Be still and know that I am God!   –Psalm 46:10

SOMETIMES, when life feels uncertain, I close my eyes for a moment and envision myself facing the shade of my Grandma's house. I lived in the cooling shadow of that tall, white farmhouse all my growing-up years as it was only a stone's throw from our sun-drenched, little house. Just thinking of Grandma's house brings a happy, secure feeling that time has not erased, even though it was torn down decades ago.

In the summertime, I would laze on the wooden, faded-green steps of our little house, facing the shade of Grandma's house, which stretched almost to my feet. Grandma always had a pie cooling in the window and through the screen, I could catch snatches of farm market reports carried on the breeze from her kitchen radio. As I drowsily warmed myself on our sun-baked steps, Grandma's brilliant orange poppies along the house foundation bobbed gently in the shade while an occasional whiff from her spearmint plants added to the all-encompassing feeling of well-being.

Along with the benevolent presence of Grandma's house, I remember the racket of blackbirds rioting in the surrounding grove, the funny sound of Grandma sneezing, Grandpa tuning his fiddle, the distant droning sounds of a tractor in the fields—while contentment settled over me like a cloak. The fresh, heavy summer air, the sky more immense than any artist could ever paint—the whole beautiful world felt contained within that still, sacred space between the two houses. To me, as a small child, heaven itself could not get any better; I felt as if I were living it on earth.

This memory reminds me of the glorious power of stillness, the joy of just being and what it is like to live from the inside out—drifting and dreaming in the flow of life's mysteries, cultivating the preciousness of small, ordinary miracles that strengthen my heart. In his best-selling classic, *Loving Yourself for God's Sake,* Adolfo Quezada says that we have been conditioned to survey our inner and outer landscapes quickly, to select the beautiful or interesting and ignore the rest. He writes, "Go beyond surface consciousness and let perception be one of experience. Allow yourself to enter the world around you. Come to respect that world—persons and things—as they are, not what you need them to be. Get out of yourself and let the world come into your heart. Hear the voice that comes from the reservoir of all experience and knowledge." In one of my favorite passages, he writes, "Listen to the silence of your spirit. Your whole self can rest in unconditional acceptance and nurturing love as the quest for knowing gives way to the security of believing. The love between yourself and God cannot be exclusively for you. It bursts from your heart into the world to do God's bidding."

When I think of the sacred, soul-filling space between my childhood home and Grandma's house, as an adult, it gives me a glimpse of what that intimate space between God and me should feel like. When you feel such deep familiarity and encompassing love, there is no end to the hope, faith and passion you can bring to the world.

God Whose Radiance Fills Every Nook and Cranny,
thank you for always reminding us so faithfully: stillness
first. Empowerment follows.

He Said

My Saturday afternoon summer ritual was mowing the lawn.
After a week in the office, I looked forward to manual labor. We
lived in the city, near a bus line and just off an interstate freeway,
so the sound of passing vehicles practically drowned out the noise
of my old gas mower. Urban life supplied an array of distractions
complete with emergency vehicle sirens, delivery vehicle beeps,
kids voices and basketball dribbling in the nearby park. A few
blocks away, heavy industry pounded away along the riverfront and
a westerly wind oftentimes carried the noise our way.

Recently while rummaging through the garage, I came across a
pair of noise protectors. While cutting the grass, I slipped them on
and something marvelous occurred—relief from the urban noise
pollution! Even though busses roared past, cars zoomed by, and
my lawn mower chattered noisily, I experienced a welcoming
silence. I breathed the world in differently. I was able to tune out
my surroundings while still being part of them. I had broken
through the "sound barrier" and found that by seeking and finding stillness and peace, I could hear the voice of my Creator.
Bypassing my sense of hearing also made me appreciate its blessing all the more.   —*JPB*

She Said

Every Wednesday is religious education night for my son. As he dashes off to class to discuss the faith he's growing in, I quietly slip into the small chapel which has perpetual adoration. On the tiny wood carved altar is the Eucharist brassy and bold, as if to say, "Here I am . . . come pray with me." Always, I try to get the kneeler next to the window, where a cocoon of radiator warmth engulfs me. While I kneel quietly, I shed the cares of the outside world, the rush of the day and the worries of tomorrow. In this space, I feel like a kindly old grandmother has scooped me up in her arms and is cradling me, smoothing her fingers across my forehead to shush the wrinkles away. I am totally at peace and no one can harm me or touch me. I am swaddled in the Lord's grace.

I pray for awhile as people shuffle in and out, only the swishing of their winter coats speak. Out of respect, there is no talking, only beautiful, calming silence. Then, I ask for God's help for my writing and time moves quickly as I read, edit, and create. Glancing at my watch, I notice that an hour has raced by. Thanking the Lord for this quiet time, I feel rejuvenated as the Bible states with "a peace that surpasses all understanding." It has centered me, calmed me and assured me that our relationship with God is key to all other relationships in both quantity and quality. —*SGB*

Work Book Page

Discussion or Journal Questions

1. I asked four friends what they thought God's message would be to those reading this book. Marci Alborghetti, author of *A Season in the South* wrote, "God is a loving parent, unlike any parent we've known or could know in this realm. His love is not constrained by the obstacles of this world. Knowing this, we may be fearless in the confidence of such a love, though never comprehending it. The message then, from our compassionate, loving parent to us is found in Jeremiah 29:11, 'For I know the plans for you, declares the Lord, plans to prosper you and not to harm you; plans to give you hope and a future.' "

   As you prepare to close this book, what comes to mind when you read that compelling biblical promise?

2. Judy Osgood, publisher of Gilgal Publications, wrote, "Spirituality is the essence of our relationship with God. Intangible but very real, that bond is the moral compass that guides our thoughts and actions. When we nurture ourselves with prayer, meditation and reading that help us to grow in our faith, we feel closer to our Heavenly Parent and better equipped to deal with life's demands. But when the responsibilities of our complex lives rob us of time for those sacred ties, uncertainty and anxieties step in to fill the gap. Ironically, 'How do I find time to develop the spiritual dimension of my life?' can be the answer as well as the question."

   Taking to heart Judy's wise words, what are some specific ways that you can incorporate deeper prayer, meditation and spiritual reading into your life?

Goal

Ann Dawson, author of *A Season of Grief* wrote, "When Mother Teresa was asked if she felt that she was a holy woman she replied that we are all called to holiness. This is not to say that we need to spend our time preaching to others about our holiness or trying to exhort others to such a state. If we live each moment of our lives in an awareness of the presence of the Divine in all we see and do, and live in the conviction that we are spirit-filled, powerful, and blessed, then holiness will fill our lives. Awareness of this divinity and the knowledge that we are co-creators with God allows us to be powerful forces of creativity, light and joy to all around us."

As your final goal, review all that you have learned and been inspired by in this book. Determine to take five of the lessons that touched you the most and revisit them often through study, prayer and reflection; vow to respond to the sacredness and action they call you to, in light of what Ann wrote.

Task

Rebecca Laird, former editor of *Sacred Journey* wrote, "the essential message for all of us is: Listen! Pay attention to the quieter messengers that will tell you the truth. The culture may have us worry about appearances, but the still, small voice of God says, 'You are enough. I made you who you are. Be my unique expression of love right where you are.' Listen to your life. You don't have to live according to other people's standards. What makes you come alive? What evil or pain in the world creates a fire in your belly? Find the people and issues that matter to you and give yourself to them. The world needs you to live in the flow of your gifts. Lastly, listen to what season it is in your life. What fueled your life at one stage of life may run empty in another. Let go and listen to what the next season is asking of you. Trust that what you have learned so far will allow you to take a new step. We are ever able to walk forward and follow, even when our steps are slowed. Perhaps this allows us to see the smaller beauties of life that are blurred in earlier seasons. All of life is a good gift if we but listen and settle in and fully live the lives we've been given."

In keeping with the prophetic words Rebecca wrote and the messages you have received in reading this book, as a final task, answer the following questions:

> **Will you say yes to Living as a Voice?**
>
> **Will you say yes to Living the Journey of Faith?**
>
> **Will you say yes to Living the Truth?**

Prayer Image

The final, sweeping benediction of the priest at Mass as he makes the sign of the cross and says, "May the Lord bless you and keep you and make his face to shine upon you and grant you peace."

Affirmation Statement

Just as I was conceived and have always lived in the heart and mind of God, I still my soul so that mutual devotion can flow freely and in turn empower me to flourish with all whom I love at the edge of God's greatness and the center of his deep, abiding embrace.

AFTERWORD

Lost Love Found

"The ring," Denise Linn writes, is described as a "powerful symbol of the continuous circle of life—a sign of completion, wholeness, unity . . . and eternal love." When my marriage fell apart, my discarded wedding rings ended up under my bed in a box, where they collected dust and were completely forgotten about.

When I moved to my apartment, I did not take my rings with me. In the year that followed, I moved through a personal evolution that was nothing short of remarkable as I processed every emotion known to humankind following the dismantling of a thirty-one-year marriage. Eventually, as I grew in personal empowerment, the trepidation gradually began to fade as I rested, prayed, studied and came to terms with the landscape of my new life—as a person living alone who was processing a divorce that I did not want. The four seasons went by and I watched the maple tree outside my window evolve from spring buds to summer lushness—to the falling of all its leaves—to the skeletal winter barren limbs. I could see a few, tenacious dried up leaves still clinging as I realized that is what hope had been like for me—a determined presence that did not let go even though my life initially felt it had ended up in a shambles at my feet, like a carpet of fallen leaves ripped away by winter winds.

Suddenly, a week before I was to sign my divorce papers, my husband and I reconciled. The day it happened, I felt flooded with the scripture verses and symbols of resurrection and redemption this book had called forth as the unexpected miracle of a second chance dawned. A future was reborn that I thought was dead, and even though it was winter, spring came alive in my heart. Despite the terrible scars that we bore, we both felt as if we were waking up from a nightmare of pain that would recede one small step at a time as we planned new lives based on trust. My wise counselor offered the words that best framed the whole experience. He wrote, *"I do not see the reconciliation as the miracle, although I am happy for both of you. I see the miracle in you and in the way you weathered the seasons and grew and developed. I see the miracle, not in the unexpected turnaround, but in the constant faith you have had in your heart that—no matter what—you would not be abandoned by God and that you would make it somehow."* His words remind all of us that we are stewards of our own peace—miracles to our own sacred hearts, whether there is reconciliation or not.

My thirty-one-year old wedding rings became symbolic of the divine grace that supported me through a continuous circle of wise people and life-changing experiences. As one era ended and another began, I understood as never before how the power of a spiritually mature heart can embrace wounds, human frailty, imperfection and mistakes through the hard work of forgiveness. Most of all, my wedding rings reminded me of the miracle of new beginnings, lost love found and the joy renewed devotion and fidelity brings.

One thing is clear. When we seek the edge of greatness in our hearts and souls, we embark upon the most sacred adventure imaginable. Three years in the writing, as I researched this book and sought to understand what coming into the fullness of one's empowerment meant, I had no idea where the journey would lead or what I would experience. I certainly did not expect the quest to include the collapse and ensuing resurrection of my marriage.

While the journey for each of us is unique and we can't know ahead of time what joys, trials, ascents and descents the road will pass through, one thing we can know for certain is that living on the edge of greatness is not a place or a destination—but rather a state of being. Like heaven, we know it is where eternal love dwells, tears are dried and the glory of God sustains us with undying devotion, passion and faithfulness. Unlike the edge of a cliff that signifies the sudden and abrupt end of a road, the edge of greatness marks the stepping-off brink to our potential in God.

It is at these very human edges that we spiritually find the edge of greatness—our precious gift from God that drops off into divine love and empowerment for living that will see us beyond any nightmares. *We awaken to the innate knowledge we were born with: we are created from greatness and it is to greatness of spirit that we are called.*

Bibliography, Resources and Recommended Books

Preface: Mentors in Hope

Macrina Wiederkehr, O.S.B., *Seasons of Your Heart: Prayers and Reflections,* Revised and Expanded (New York, NY: HarperCollins Publishers, 1991).

Adolfo Quezada, *Loving Yourself for God's Sake* (Totowa, NJ: Resurrection Press, 1997).

May Sarton, "Now I Become Myself" (St. Meinrad Archabbey, IN: CareNote from One Caring Place, 1988).

Part One: Living as a Voice

The Ugly Duckling: Living Powerfully

Clarissa Pinkola Estes, Ph.D., *Women Who Run with the Wolves: Myths and Stories of the Wild Woman Archetype* (New York, NY: Ballatine Books, Random House, 1992).

Thomas Moore, *Care of the Soul: A Guide for Cultivating Depth and Sacredness in Everyday Life* (New York, NY: HarperCollins Publishers, Inc., 1992).

Beyond the Silence

Joseph Campbell, *The Power of Myth: With Bill Moyers* (New York, NY: Anchor Books, Doubleday, 1988).

Sr. Ave Clark, O.P., *Lights in the Darkness: For Survivors and Healers of Sexual Abuse* (Totowa, NJ: Resurrection Press, 1993).

Sacred Space on the Internet

Julia Cameron, *The Artist's Way: A Spiritual Path to Higher Creativity* (New York, NY: The Putman Publishing Group, 1992).

Patricia H. Livingston, *This Blessed Mess: Finding Hope Amidst Life's Chaos* (Notre Dame, IN: Ave Maria Press, Sorin Books, 2000).

Christiane Northrup, M.D., *Women's Bodies, Women's Wisdom: Creating Physical and Emotional Health* (New York, NY: Bantam Doubleday Dell Publishing Group, Inc., 1994).

Blessed Be the Peacemakers

Marie Therese Archambault, *A Retreat With Black Elk: Living in the Sacred Hoop* (Cincinnati, OH: St. Anthony Messenger Press, 1998).

Kent Nerburn, *Small Graces: The Quiet Gifts of Everyday Life* (Novato, CA: New World Library, 1998).

War Through the Eyes of A Child

Adolfo Quezada, Desert Spirit, February, 2003.

Adolfo Quezada, *Walking with God: Reflecting on Life's Meaning* (Ligouri, MO: Liguori Publications, 1990).

Antoinette Bosco, *Choosing Mercy: A Mother of Murder Victims Pleads to End the Death Penalty* (Maryknoll, NY: Orbis Books, 2001).

The Legacy of a Leopard Coat

Christin Lore Weber, *Circle of Mysteries: The Women's Rosary Book* (St. Paul, MN: Yes International Publishers, 1995).

Walking in Fog

Barbara Kingsolver, *Small Wonder: Essays* (New York, NY: Perennial, HarperCollins Publishers Inc., 2002).

A Chicken Named Elvis

Jean Shinoda Bolen, M.D., *Goddesses in Older Women: Archetypes in Women Over Fifty, Becoming a Juicy Crone* (New York, NY: Quill, HarperCollins Publishers Inc., 2001).

Ann Dawson, *A Season of Grief: A Comforting Companion for Difficult Days* (Notre Dame, IN: Ave Maria Press, 2002).

Melannie Svoboda, S.N.D., *Everyday Epiphanies: Seeing the Sacred in Every Thing* (Mystic, CT: Twenty-Third Publications, 1997).

Part Two: Living the Journey of Faith

Fear, Faith and a Snake

Sue Monk Kidd, *The Secret Life of Bees: A Novel* (New York, NY: Viking Penguin, 2002).

Denise Linn, *The Secret Language of Signs: How to Interpret the Coincidences and Symbols in Your Life* (New York, NY: Ballantine Books, 1996).

What Our Hearts Become

Ann Dawson, *A Season of Grief: A Comforting Companion for Difficult Days* (Notre Dame, IN: Ave Maria Press, 2002).

Sam Keen, *Hymns to an Unknown God: Awakening the Spirit in Everyday Life* (New York, NY: Bantam Books, 1994).

Joyce Rupp, *Your Sorrow Is My Sorrow: Hope and Strength in Times of Suffering* (New York, NY: The Crossroad Publishing Company, 1999).

A Living Compass

Adolfo Quezada, *Rising From the Ashes: A Month of Prayer to Heal Our Wounds* (Totowa, NJ: Resurrection Press, 2002).

The Optimist Challenge

Martin E.P. Seligman, Ph.D., T*he Optimistic Child: A Proven Program to Safeguard Children Against Depression and Build Lifelong Resilience* (New York, NY: Harper Perennial, HarperCollins Publishers, 1995).

Paul Rogat Loeb, *Soul of a Citizen: Living with Conviction in a Cynical Time* (New York, NY: St. Martin's Press, 1999).

Macrina Wiederkehr, *Gold in Your Memories: Sacred Moments, Glimpses of God* (Notre Dame, IN: Ave Maria Press, 1998).

The Colors of Life

Madeleine L'Engle, *The Rock That is Higher: Story as Truth* (Wheaton, IL: Harold Shaw Publishers, 1993).

Denise Linn, *The Secret Language of Signs: How to Interpret the Coincidences and Symbols in Your Life* (New York, NY: Ballantine Books, 1996).

Gregory F.A. Pierce, *Spirituality @ Work: 10 Ways to Balance Your Life on the Job* (Chicago, IL: Loyola Press, 2001).

Woman on Walkabout

Marlo Morgan, *Mutant Messages Down Under* (New York, NY: Harper Perennial, 1995).

Adolfo Quezada, S*abbath Moments: Finding Rest for the Soul in the Midst of Daily Living* (Totowa, NJ: Resurrection Press, 2003).

A Tribute to a Mother-in-Law

Ann Dawson, *A Season of Grief: A Comforting Companion for Difficult Days* (Notre Dame, IN: Ave Maria Press, 2002).

Part Three: Living the Truth

Beyond Hatred

Mitch Albom, *Tuesdays With Morrie: An Old Man, A Young Man, and Life's Greatest Lesson* (New York, NY: Broadway Books, Random House, 1997).

Sue Monk Kidd, *The Secret Life of Bees: A Novel* (NewYork, NY: Viking Penguin, 2002).

Barbara Kingsolver, *Small Wonder: Essays* (New York, NY: Perennial, HarperCollins Publishers Inc., 2002).

Incubation

Gertrude Mueller Nelson, *To Dance With God: Family Ritual and Community Celebration* (Mahwah, NJ: Paulist Press, 1986).

Sue Monk Kidd, *Dance of the Dissident Daughter: A Woman's Journey from Christian Tradition to the Sacred Feminine* (NewYork, NY: HarperCollinsPublishers, 1996).

The Final Lesson

Dr. Richard Johnson, ALAM, June, 2002.

The Shadow of Depression

Dr. Robert Thompson, Reprinted with permission from Bereavement Publishing, Inc., 888-604-4673.

Telling Our Stories

Larry Woiwode, editors Mark Vinz, Thom Tammaro, *Inheriting the Land: Contemporary Voices from the Midwest* (Minneapolis, MN: U of M Press, 1993).

Living the Miracle

Julia Cameron, *The Artist's Way: A Spiritual Path to Higher Creativity* (New York, NY: The Putman Publishing Group, 1992).

Macrina Wiederkehr, *Behold Your Life: A Pilgrimage Through Your Memories* (Notre Dame, IN: Ave Maria Press, 1999).

Joseph Campbell, *The Power of Myth: With Bill Moyers* (New York, NY: Anchor Books, Doubleday, 1988).

The Glory That is God

Christin Lore Weber, *Circle of Mysteries: The Women's Rosary Book* (St. Paul, MN: Yes International Publishers, 1995).

The Glory of Stillness

Adolfo Quezada, *Loving Yourself for God's Sake* (Totowa, NJ: Resurrection Press, 1997).

Titles You Might Enjoy

OTHER BOOKS OF INTEREST

MEDITATIONS FOR SURVIVORS OF SUICIDE

Joni Woelfel

". . . leaves us with a conviction that survivors of suicide can truly live again with courage, hope and a new resurrection." —Antoinette Bosco

". . . an accessible and truly comforting book. I wholeheartedly recommend this inspiring resource for anyone surviving the suicide of a loved one, or indeed for anyone who grieves.'" —Amy Florian

No. RP 170/04 ISBN 1-878718-75-4 **$8.95**

SABBATH MOMENTS

Adolfo Quezada

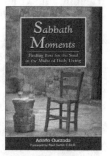

A six-week psalter format using Scripture, reflection, and prayer to soothe your mind, body and soul. By becoming conscious of God in Sabbath Moments, we rest, restore and re-create ourselves.

No. RP 178/04 ISBN 1-878718-80-0 **$6.95**

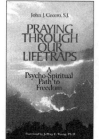

PRAYING THROUGH OUR LIFETRAPS

John J. Cecero, S.J.

"John Cecero's unique book can be read not only as a primer on lifetrap therapy and practice but as a spiritual guide to finding God in all things." —Joseph R. Novello, M.D.

No. RP 164/04 ISBN 1-878718-70-3 **$9.95**

LIFE, LOVE AND LAUGHTER

Father Jim Vlaun

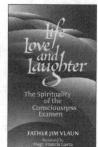

"Within only a few pages, you know you're in the company of a truly good man, someone with a big heart whose feet are firmly on the ground, . . . There is so much simple, shining wisdom in this book." —William J. O'Malley, S.J.

No. RP 113/04 ISBN 1-878718-43-6 **$7.95**

www.catholicbookpublishing.com

Additional Titles Published by Resurrection Press, a Catholic Book Publishing Imprint

A Rachel Rosary *Larry Kupferman*	$4.50
A Season in the South *Marci Alborghetti*	$10.95
Blessings All Around *Dolores Leckey*	$8.95
Catholic Is Wonderful *Mitch Finley*	$4.95
Days of Intense Emotion *Keeler/Moses*	$12.95
Discernment *Chris Aridas*	$8.95
Feasts of Life *Jim Vlaun*	$12.95
From Holy Hour to Happy Hour *Francis X. Gaeta*	$7.95
Grace Notes *Lorraine Murray*	$9.95
Healing through the Mass *Robert DeGrandis, SSJ*	$9.95
Our Grounds for Hope *Fulton J. Sheen*	$7.95
Healing Your Grief *Ruthann Williams, OP*	$7.95
Heart Peace *Adolfo Quezada*	$9.95
How Shall We Pray? *James Gaffney*	$5.95
Lessons for Living from the 23rd Psalm *Victor Parachin*	$5.95
The Joy of Being an Altar Server *Joseph Champlin*	$5.95
The Joy of Being a Catechist *Gloria Durka*	$4.95
The Joy of Being a Eucharistic Minister *Mitch Finley*	$5.95
The Joy of Being a Lector *Mitch Finley*	$5.95
The Joy of Being an Usher *Gretchen Hailer, RSHM*	$5.95
The Joy of Marriage Preparation *McDonough/Marinelli*	$5.95
The Joy of Music Ministry *J.M. Talbot*	$6.95
The Joy of Praying the Rosary *James McNamara*	$5.95
The Joy of Preaching *Rod Damico*	$6.95
The Joy of Teaching *Joanmarie Smith*	$5.95
The Joy of Worshiping Together *Rod Damico*	$5.95
Lights in the Darkness *Ave Clark, O.P.*	$8.95
Loving Yourself for God's Sake *Adolfo Quezada*	$5.95
Magnetized by God *Robert E. Lauder*	$8.95
Meditations for Survivors of Suicide *Joni Woelfel*	$8.95
Mother Teresa *Eugene Palumbo, S.D.B.*	$5.95
Mourning Sickness *Keith Smith*	$8.95
Personally Speaking *Jim Lisante*	$8.95
Prayers from a Seasoned Heart *Joanne Decker*	$8.95
Praying the Lord's Prayer with Mary *Muto/vanKaam*	$8.95
5-Minute Miracles *Linda Schubert*	$4.95
Sabbath Moments *Adolfo Quezada*	$6.95
Season of New Beginnings *Mitch Finley*	$4.95
Season of Promises *Mitch Finley*	$4.95
Sometimes I Haven't Got a Prayer *Mary Sherry*	$8.95
St. Katharine Drexel *Daniel McSheffery*	$12.95
What He Did for Love *Francis X. Gaeta*	$5.95
Woman Soul *Pat Duffy, OP*	$7.95
You Are My Beloved *Mitch Finley*	$10.95

For a free catalog call 1-800-892-6657
www.catholicbookpublishing.com